TechCareers:

Biomedical Equipment Technicians

Dr. Roger Bowles

Texas State Technical College Waco

TSTC Publishing™

© 2008 TSTC Publishing

ISBN 978-1-934302-29-3

TSTC Publishing
Texas State Technical College Waco
3801 Campus Drive
Waco, Texas 76705

http://publishing.tstc.edu/

Publisher: Mark Long
Project Manager: Grace Arsiaga
Printing production: Bill Evridge
Graphics Specialist: Stacie Buterbaugh
Index: Michelle Gray
        indexing@yahoo.com

Manufactured in the United States of America

First edition

Table of Contents

Chapter 1 – Biomedical Equipment Technician Careers **1**

  BMET Overview 1

  Employment Outlook 4

  Salary Ranges 7

  Career Paths 10

  Job Titles 11

  Job Duties 13

  Work Schedules 15

  Employers 17

  Necessary Skill Sets. 23

  Conclusion 34

Chapter 2 – Biomedical Equipment Technician Education &

Certification **37**

  Educational Requirements 39

  The Two-Year Associate of Applied Science Degree 41

  The Four-Year Bachelor's Degree 42

  Tuition and Fees. 44

  BMET Certification 48

  CBET Certification 51

  Dialysis Certification for BMETs 53

  Computer Certifications 54

  Continuing Education 57

  Conclusion 59

Chapter 3 – Additional Biomedical Equipment Technician

Information & Resources. **61**

  BMET Higher Education Programs in the United States . . 61

  BMET Two- and Four-Year Degree Plans 79

BMET Employers, Equipment Manufacturers

& Recruiters 91

BMET Associations 96

BMET Industry Publications 99

Additional Suggested Resources 100

Index **103**

About the Author **107**

TSTC Publishing **109**

Acknowledgments

This book would not have been possible without the very important contributions of the following people who conducted interviews to produce the profiles and related materials: Clay Coppedge (employers), Helen Ginger (technicians), Heather Lee (students) and Karen Mitchell Smith (instructors).

In addition, special thanks are due to TSTC Emerging Technologies under the direction of Michael Bettersworth, Associate Vice Chancellor for Technology Advancement, who provided financial underwriting to make this project possible.

Dr. Roger Bowles

Commonly Used Abbreviations

AAMI   Association for the Advancement of Medical
Instrumentation

A.A.S.   Associate of Applied Science

BMET   Biomedical Equipment Technician

B.S.   Bachelor of Science

CBET   Certified Biomedical Equipment Technician

CLES   Certified Laboratory Equipment Specialist

CRES   Certified Radiology Equipment Specialist

CT   Computerized Tomography

DICOM   Digital Imaging and Communications in
Medicine

ICC   International Certification Commission

ISO   Independent Service Organization

IT   Information Technology

IUPUI   Purdue University and Indiana University
campus

FDA   Food and Drug Administration

OEM   Original Equipment Manufacturer

OSHA   Occupational Safety and Health Administration

MCSE   Microsoft Certified Systems Engineer

MIT   Medical Imaging Systems Technology

MRI   Magnetic Resonance Imaging

MSA   Middle States Association of Schools and
Colleges

NCA   North Central Association of Schools

NEASC   New England Association of Schools and
Colleges

NWCCU   Northwest Commission on Colleges and
Universities

PACS   Picture Archiving and Communication Systems

PM   Preventive Maintenance

RFID   Radio Frequency Identification

SACS   Southern Association of Colleges and Schools

UHS   Universal Hospital Services

WASC   Western Association of Schools and Colleges

Chapter 1: Biomedical Equipment Technician Careers

People choose the field they go into for many reasons: sometimes for money, sometimes for stability and sometimes for the satisfaction of helping others. The reasons given for selecting biomedical equipment technician as a career choice, then, encompass all these and more.

Biomedical equipment technicians (BMETs) are responsible for the maintenance, repair and calibration of medical electronic equipment found in hospitals, including ventilators, infusion pumps, patient monitors, defibrillators and ultrasound machines. Professional BMETs on the job say the job is challenging, rewarding and ever-changing. Networking, continuing education and a willingness to work with people as well as the equipment are key parts of the job.

BMET Overview

Medical equipment has been around for hundreds, if not thousands, of years, and it has evolved from crude sharpened pieces of wood used for bloodletting and chipped stone knives used for trepanning (removing depressed skull fractures) to the Gamma knife and the ultramodern CyberKnife used in radiosurgery to treat deep-seated brain tumors and other previously untreatable conditions. Over the past 40 to 50 years, medical devices used to diagnose, monitor and treat patients have undergone an extraordinary evolution. Today's healthcare facilities have millions of dollars worth of medical electronic devices, including X-ray machines, ultrasound scanners, patient monitors, ventilators and infusion pumps. This equipment, although highly reliable and safe, does require maintenance, repair and calibration. The biomedical equipment technology field consists of professionals who do just that.

Biomedical equipment technology, relatively speaking, is still a very young field. It was "born" in the mid 1960s and early 1970s because of a concern for patient safety with the increasing use of electronic medical equipment in hospitals. In 1969, Dr. Carl Walter of Peter Bent Brigham hospital in Boston shocked the nation by reporting that stray electrical currents in hospital medical equipment were inducing ventricular defibrillation in patients. Ventricular fibrillation is a condition in which the heart loses its own natural rhythm and quivers uncontrollably like a bag of worms. This condition, if not corrected, rapidly leads to death. These stray electrical currents, most so small as not to be felt by the average healthy person, were electrocuting sick patients connected to medical devices, some 1,200 per year according to Walter. He was not alone in his concern. Consumer advocate Ralph Nader thought Walter's estimate was conservative and published an article in the *Ladies Home Journal* in 1971 stating the real number of accidental electrocutions in hospitals was closer to 5,000. Others followed suit with estimates as high as 12,000 per year. These reports led to the formation of safety standards for electro-medical equipment and the need for technicians to check, maintain and repair these devices.

Electrical safety isn't the problem it used to be. Today's medical devices are safer and more reliable than ever. However, they continue to grow in complexity. Medical equipment, like expensive cars, still malfunctions and still needs to be checked for proper performance and regularly maintained. In the 1960s, the few people trained to work on medical electronic equipment mostly worked for equipment manufacturers. Very few hospitals had personnel on staff to do this job, and training programs were almost non-existent with the exception of the military.

Today, biomedical equipment technology is still a small field with an estimated 30,000 to 50,000 technicians nationwide, but it is growing rapidly as equipment becomes more complex and the population ages and requires more and more healthcare. Chances are if you ask the average person on the street who maintains medical equipment in hospitals, he or she will have no idea. Indeed, even if you are a regular follower of television medical dramas such as *House, ER* or *Grey's Anatomy*, you have probably never seen an episode that shows anyone running to repair the last available ventilator or even mentions the reliability of the equipment at all. Nevertheless, biomedical equipment technicians have been called the "Special Forces of High Tech Healthcare" with an essential role in today's healthcare system. And although much of their work goes on behind the scenes, they are an integral part of the professional healthcare team and critical to patient safety and positive treatment outcome.

A career in biomedical equipment technology will be a rewarding one, not only financially and for job security, but also for the challenges and opportunities it will provide. It also provides a very rare sense of job satisfaction—a feeling of accomplishment at the end of the day, knowing you make a real difference in the diagnosis and treatment of patients and in the work of other healthcare professionals.

Employment Outlook

The outlook is very bright for the medical equipment service industry and according to the Occupational Outlook Handbook and professional recruiters, the demand for individuals in this field will remain strong in the future. Reasons that demand for skilled technicians will continue to outweigh the supply include:

- Aging of current workers in the profession will bring increased opportunities as these workers retire. According to a recent survey in the Journal of Clinical Engineering, the average age is 42.

- Aging of the general population will mean increased need for medical treatment and therefore more equipment needs as "baby boomers" reach retirement age.

- Lack of publicity about this field among high school graduates and their counselors will continue to mean a shortage of "new blood."

- Increasing opportunities as technologies blend and evolve.

Job stability also appeals to many entering the field. Fifty-two percent of survey respondents in the trade magazine *24x7* report having been with their current employer for 16 or more years, an impressive figure in a world where the average person stays in a technical job for 13 months.

BMET Profile: Robert Davis

Davis came to his career as a BMET relatively late in life

He was hurt in a traffic accident in 1991 after working for the better part of 20 years in the petrochemical and pharmaceutical industries. "I was finally just tired of sitting around and this kind of work looked like the best thing for me," he says.

Having worked for two decades before entering the field, Davis brings some experience and insight into the education of a BMET and how that plays out in the real world. That so much of the equipment is computer- and network-driven gave him "a big learning curve," he says. "It's becoming even more dominant in the field."

He urges students to work an internship at a hospital while studying in the classroom. "You learn how a hospital works," he says. "You get to see how different departments work together. It's one thing to study it in a classroom, but you don't really know what it's like until you live it."

Davis oversees equipment at Crest, an independent service organization that contracts with hospitals, which basically leaves him in charge of more than 2,000 pieces of medical equipment. "There's so much medical equipment that you can't know it all," he says. "You have to evolve as you work and be able to adapt to every little thing that comes up."

After two years working as a BMET, Davis knows he made the right choice when he chose the life of a BMET. Dealing with the people in the hospital has proved to be an unexpected bonus for him. From his previous jobs, he was used to working with people with all kinds of personality types.

"When I started out, I thought I'd just be dealing with machines, fixing boxes," he says. "Mechanically, it didn't seem all that hard. You do some troubleshooting—which can be pretty intense—but most of the time you know what to do when you start."

That's where knowing how to work with people comes in handy, he says. "I like working with the people," he says. "I like the whole hospital setting. I know the people's names and they know mine, and you get to know the people as you go along."

"But the key to continuing success in the field is continuing education," he says. He hopes to have a directorship in the next five to ten years and toward that end is beginning work to get his bachelor's degree.

It's a business that will continue to need qualified workers, Davis continues. "We can't fill all the spots we have now," he says. "Not all of them are entry level jobs. There's a demand for the higher level spots, too. It's going to take someone with more than an associate's degree.

"This is really a great field to get into," he concludes. "It's the best job I've ever had."

BMET Repairing Ventilator

Salary Ranges

Earnings for biomedical equipment technicians, specialists and field service representatives vary according to employer, location and the training and the individual technician's educational background. Typical starting salaries for entry-level technicians in 2007 have ranged from $32,000 to $42,000 annually in the South Central United States. Larger hospitals and ISOs, as well as manufacturers, usually have higher pay scales. Individuals working in larger cities also typically earn more, as do those specializing (such as medical imaging specialists). Those individuals entering the field with skills learned in other areas such as electronics, computers or management also typically start at higher rates than those with no work background. Former military personnel also usually land higher salaries starting out.

After three to five years of experience, BMETs can expect to make $42,000 to $50,000 annually and $50,000 to $70,000 after five to seven years of experience, depending on training and background. Medical imaging specialists with several years of experience in a modality such as CT or MR can expect earnings of over $70,000 annually. Department directors and account managers can make $80,000 to $120,000 per year depending on their employer, location and responsibilities.

Entry-level technicians starting out as field service representatives for manufacturers usually earn more than those beginning with ISOs or in-house departments, with starting salaries of $42,000 and up annually not uncommon. Experienced field service representatives may move up to become regional managers or even national service managers and earn salaries over $100,000 per year.

On-call pay for biomedical equipment technicians working in-house or for ISOs ranges from $1 per hour to over $4 per hour, just for being on call after hours. The typical number of hours on call in a week is about 128, so this can mean anywhere from $128 to $512 extra. If a technician is called in on an emergency, he or she normally receives time and a half pay for the time spent at the hospital and travel. Some hospitals and companies have minimum number of hours for call back pay established (so if the employer has a minimum four-hour policy, that means the technician gets paid for four hours even if the repair only takes one hour). BMETs usually rotate being on call with other members of the department or company with one week of on call every four to six weeks being common. Field service representatives working for a manufacturer typically do not get on-call pay and are on call twenty-four hours per day, seven days per week, unless relieved by a another field service representative from another coverage area.

Biomedical equipment technicians and field service representatives usually have medical benefits through their employer. Many employers pay all of the cost for the employee, and some even pay the cost for both the employee and family (although this is rare). Most employers also provide a retirement plan, and many offer tuition reimbursement if the technician wants to pursue a four-year degree or even a graduate degree. Tuition reimbursement is becoming a key benefit in an age in which lifelong learning is becoming the norm.

Most employers also provide two weeks of paid vacation and at least six paid holidays. Some start with three weeks of vacation. Technicians expected to travel in their job are usually either provided a company car or they are paid a monthly allowance to compensate for their expenses. Other benefits (not as common) might include the use of an onsite fitness center or fitness center membership, onsite child care and profit sharing.

BMET Profile: Heather Fleming

Like Robert Davis, Fleming likes her job. She works at Memorial Hospital in Lufkin, Texas as an imaging repair specialist, repairing general hospital radiology equipment. "I like it better than I thought I would," she says. "Halfway through my studies I kind of got impatient and just wanted to get out there and start working. When I did, I liked it better than I thought I would."

Learning to deal with the stress that comes with the job is important not only in enjoying the job but also being able to do it. "Sometimes a piece of equipment will break down and you have to fix it right then and there, because a patient is an emergency status. You have to learn to just step back, take a deep breath and just go in there and do it."

To get used to the pace and pressure of a hospital or clinic setting, Fleming advises students to get work in a hospital, even if it's not as an intern. "Just work anywhere in a hospital," she says. "You get used to the pace, to the terminology. You get to see how a hospital operates. It's not so intimidating if you've been around it."

Because the BMET field is so diverse, Fleming advises paying close attention to everything that comes up in the classroom. "You're going to need to know some anatomy and physiology," she says. "It helps you learn what certain equipment is used for. There are five different kinds of blood pressure machines you might have to work on. Knowing how the body operates helps you understand how the equipment operates."

Technology is moving quickly, and it pays the ambitious BMET to stay up with the latest trends and developments. Nearly everything now, Fleming says, is digital. Much of that technology has come along after she graduated from Texas State Technical College Waco. "I learned a lot of it pretty much on the job," she says.

Along with changing technology is an increasing demand for BMETs. "There's always going to be a need for it," she says. "Networking becomes more and more important as the job field opens up."

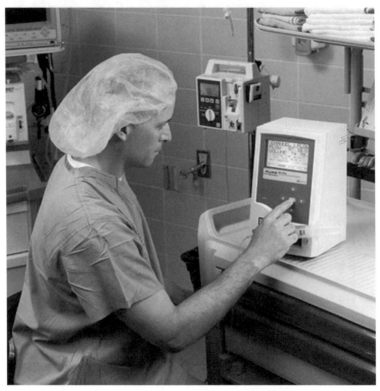

BMET Using Infusion Pump Analyzer to Test Pump in Surgery

Career Paths

Career paths for biomedical equipment technicians and field service representatives vary according to the type and size of employer and with the preferences of the individual. A biomedical equipment technician might start off his or her career as a BMET I, then advance to a BMET II after two to three years, then to a BMET III after five to 10 years. He or she might decide to specialize in a certain area like radiology, anesthesia or laboratory after a few years and become a BMET specialist or become a BMET supervisor. In a smaller hospital or ISO, a technician might have limited options for advancement or specialization. In larger healthcare systems or ISOs, the opportunities for advancement and specialization are usually greater, but sometimes advancing or specializing involves changing locations. Sometimes it also involves changing employers. More formal education, such as the completion of a bachelor's degree, can open up management opportunities such as department director (in-house), account manager or regional manager (ISO and OEM). Some technicians choose to stay generalists while others choose to specialize. Still others move into IT related areas such as PACS (Picture Archiving and Communication Systems) administration or perhaps a BMET/IT liaison technician. Other avenues might include facilities management, risk management, medical equipment sales or even starting a business as an ISO.

Job Titles

Individuals working in the field of biomedical equipment technology have a variety of different titles depending on their employer, specialization or level of experience. One of the most common titles is biomedical equipment technician or BMET for short. Variations of this include biomedical electronics technician, biomedical engineering technician, clinical engineering technician, or medical equipment repair technician. BMETs may be generalists working on a wide variety of equipment, or they may specialize in one or two types of equipment or "modalities." A BMET may specialize in respiratory therapy equipment, anesthesia equipment, sterilizers, ultrasound, monitoring equipment, dialysis equipment, laboratory equipment or others.

Individuals specializing in imaging equipment such as X-ray, computerized tomography (CT), magnetic resonance imaging (MRI) equipment or radiation therapy equipment (cancer treatment) are often called radiology equipment specialists, medical imaging specialists or X-ray repair specialists.

BMET Profile: Billy Andrews

Learning to ask questions in class not only helps in college but also on the job, according to Billy Andrews, who works in-house at a hospital for an independent service organization (ISO). Just as there are things you won't know in the classroom, you're going to run across unfamiliar situations on the job, he says.

"Don't be afraid to ask questions," he suggests. "TSTC introduces students to the most common things in the hospital but not everything. It has happened to me where I have been called to look at something and had no clue what it does. By asking the operators how they use it and what's not working for them, I can take the information, and my understanding of system troubleshooting, and have a good chance at solving their problem."

Like the other BMETs profiled in this chapter, Andrews advises students to get a job in a hospital while they're studying. "They should volunteer at the local hospital," he says. "It will give them additional experience in the hospital environment."

Once he graduated from TSTC, Andrews had something of a crash course in the realities of the working world. He expected to enter at an entry level and do entry-level duties. "But in my case I was asked to do much more," he says. "After attending the DACUM meeting at TSTC, I found from the other techs it was pretty much the same for them, maybe not to the same extent, but it was pretty much the same experience."

The interplay between people and machines works both ways, he says. While he says that customer service—working with the staff—is the hardest part of the job, it still isn't that bad. "Granted, you might run into a tough equipment problem on occasion, but you will have customer service obstacles to navigate daily," he says.

"What I like is most everything. I love electronics, and you can't beat the environment. What I like least is that I didn't start in this field sooner."

Job Duties

Biomedical Equipment Technicians maintain, adjust, calibrate and repair the medical equipment used by physicians, nurses and allied healthcare personnel to diagnose, monitor and treat patients at healthcare facilities. They also check the equipment for proper operation and safety using many types of unique test equipment, including patient simulators, defibrillator analyzers, electrical safety analyzers, infusion pump analyzers, electrosurgical unit analyzers, pressure meters, X-ray kVp meters and conductivity meters. Take a look at www.onestopbiomedshop.com and www.flukebiomedical.com for examples of the many types of test equipment used by BMETs. BMETs also use common test equipment such as digital volt meters, oscilloscopes and photo tachometers to troubleshoot and diagnose equipment problems.

In addition to performing preventive maintenance and repair, BMETs often train hospital staff on the proper usage and safety of medical equipment. Operator error accounts for a large portion of equipment service calls, and BMETs must not only know how to maintain and repair the equipment but also know its proper operation as well.

Biomedical equipment technicians perform a variety of other duties, such as serving on a hospital's safety committee. They may do research and recommend or advise against equipment purchases. When medical equipment is involved in the injury or death of a patient, BMETs are often involved in the investigation of the equipment and help determine the cause of the incident and how to prevent future problems. BMETs working in-house and for ISOs may coordinate warranty work by field service representatives and serve as the contact point when manufacturers are called for service issues. Most Biomedical or Clinical Engineering Departments also maintain an inventory of parts on-hand so "mission critical" equipment such as X-ray machines, ventilators and patient monitors can be repaired immediately. BMETs also coordinate services with information technology (IT) personnel to determine whether equipment failures are related to hospital network problems or with the medical equipment itself. BMETs might also check the performance of networks using network analyzers, protocol analyzers, Wi-Fi spectrum analyzers and cable testers.

At the beginning of their careers, BMETs typically perform more preventive maintenance duties than repairs. As they gain more expertise, the balance shifts and they perform more repair work than preventive maintenance. After a technician has worked for an employer for several months or maybe even a year, he or she will often be sent to manufacturers' training schools for specialized training on specific equipment. This training is often negotiated into the purchase of the equipment by the hospital. Upon return, the technician is considered the resident expert on that particular equipment and is often required to train other technicians in the department on the basics of maintenance and repair of that equipment, as well as common problems encountered. Some employers require technicians to sign a one or two year contract before going to manufacturers' training stating that if they leave before the contract expires, then the money spent by the employer on the training school must be repaid.

The job duties section would not be complete without mention of customer service. Customer service is one of the most important (some say *the* most important) duties of a biomedical equipment technician or field service representative and can often be the determining factor in the reputation of the technician, the department and/or the company. Customer service involves listening to the customer, understanding the customer and providing mutually acceptable solutions to the customer in a positive, professional and timely manner. This means answering the phone immediately and professionally, responding to the customer's needs and following up to ensure customer satisfaction. In the healthcare environment, the customer is ultimately the patient, but for biomedical equipment technicians, the most immediate customers are usually the nurses, doctors and staff using the equipment. Even if a piece of equipment is repaired and returned, if the user isn't satisfied, then the problem isn't solved.

Work Schedules

Most BMETs work a regular 40-hour work week with occasional overtime for emergencies or for scheduled preventive maintenance during light use hours for certain areas of the hospital such as surgery or radiology. Typical hours are from 8 a.m. to 5 p.m., Monday through Friday, although some technicians may work from 6 a.m. to 3 p.m. or even second shift hours from 1 p.m. to 10 p.m., depending on their employer. Most BMETs also serve periods of "on call" time where they must respond to emergencies after hours and on weekends. On call is usually rotated, and BMETs typically get paid extra just for being on call. If they are called in for an emergency, BMETs are usually compensated for that as well.

Field service representatives working for a manufacturer have varied hours and may be on call at all times. They may work 20 hours one week and 80 hours the next. Some are on salary while others work on a hybrid hourly system where they are paid for 40 hours per week regardless if they work a few hours fewer but receive overtime for over 40 hours. Field service reps also tend to travel more if their territories are large. Territories are often determined by the amount of their employer's equipment located in a certain geographic region. Some field service representatives might only cover a metro area while others cover several states.

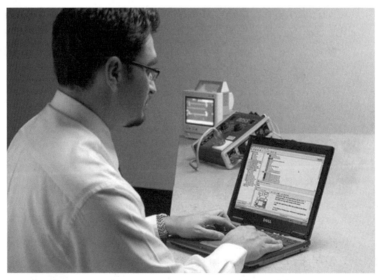

Testing Patient Monitor

Employers

Employers of medical imaging and biomedical equipment technicians will tell you that learning doesn't stop after graduating from college. Even after you achieve your certification (if you choose to become certified) and have been in the field for years as a senior BMET or senior imaging tech, there are schematics to study, new equipment to research, skills to perfect and people to help. That is what makes the biomedical equipment / imaging field fascinating — it is neither mundane nor boring.

Ken Swartz, manager of digital imaging support with Hologic, Inc., started his career before cell phones and laptops. After graduating from the Franklin Institute in Boston with a BMET degree, he had to handwrite all his service reports. "I have been in this field for 30 years now, and every day is a new day. New problems, new challenges. The technology is changing so rapidly that it forces you to keep current. It's an exciting time. I have been fortunate to be on the development teams of cutting edge technology," he said.

What might surprise some people is that being a biomedical engineer or medical imaging technician requires more than expertise at repairing or refurbishing the wide array of machines used in hospitals, clinics and the medical field in general. A BMET is expected to work well with doctors, nurses, patients and administrators. Andrew Stiles, director of clinical engineering services at St. Joseph Regional Health Center, said he would rather have "a person who's excellent at communicating than have someone who's more technical but can't communicate." When it comes to dealing with the customers (anyone the technician interacts with during the day), Stiles said it's important "to learn body language, the tone of their voice, how they speak to you and the ways they like to be communicated to, whether it's verbal, written, informal or formal communication." Although technical proficiency is very important, employers like Stiles and Swartz look for more than just a high GPA.

In addition to technical skills, a BMET needs to work both alone and as a team player with other techs in a hospital or healthcare facility. However, most of a tech's time will be spent working solo under urgent and stressful conditions. The BMET must prioritize, analyze and react on his own. Scott Sovocool, director of biomedical engineering services for Methodist Health System in Dallas, said that when interviewing people, he looks for "self-starters, who can intentionally manage their day-to-day work without a lot of extra supervision." A word used often by employers of biomedical equipment / imaging techs is "proactive." They look for people who take the initiative to get things done or who, on their own, do the extra work or the necessary studying. They don't have to be micromanaged, or, as one employer put it, "babysat."

All the employers interviewed had three things in common: they work hard, they have advanced far in their careers and they love what they do. Not a bad testimonial for biomedical equipment and imaging techs about to graduate and begin working in the field.

BMETs and specialists most commonly work at hospitals, medical centers and other types of healthcare facilities. Technicians employed by a hospital or healthcare system are often called "in-house" technicians and they typically work in a biomedical or clinical engineering department with other in-house technicians. Some work for other departments within the hospital such as surgery, radiology, or respiratory therapy. It is important to note that in some hospitals, biomedical or clinical engineering departments fall under the category of facilities maintenance or engineering. However, more and more biomedical or clinical engineering departments are a part of the information technology (IT) department as medical equipment is increasingly networked together with other modalities and functions, both inside and outside the hospital, through the Internet.

Other technicians work for independent service organizations (ISOs) or multi-vendor service providers that contract with hospitals and other healthcare organizations to provide equipment services and technology management services. These independent service organizations are sometimes referred to as "third-party" organizations and range in size from one or two employees in a local area to over a thousand employees spread across the nation. A technician working for an ISO may work at several smaller hospitals in a small or large geographic area or at one large hospital with other ISO technicians. Examples of larger, nationwide ISOs include Aramark, Masterplan and GE Healthcare (GE has an ISO subdivision in addition to being a manufacturer of several types of medical equipment). Crest Services, Trimedx, Universal Hospital Services (UHS) and Trimedx are also national ISOs. More ISO examples are provided at the end of this book.

Some technicians work for medical equipment manufacturers, sometimes referred to as original equipment manufacturers (OEMs), as field service representatives. Field service representatives may also be referred to as field service engineers, customer engineers or field service technicians. Field service representatives may work in a large or small geographic area servicing a particular type of equipment manufactured by their employer. They may perform warranty work or the hospital may have a service contract with the manufacturer to maintain and repair specific equipment as needed. Field service representatives often work out of their home and may be provided with a company car. Examples of medical equipment manufacturers include Hologic, General Electric, Dräger Medical, Siemens, Toshiba and Spacelabs. More manufacturers are listed at the end of the book.

Other employers of biomedical equipment technicians include dialysis clinics (i.e. Fresenius Medical Care, DaVita), durable medical equipment providers (home healthcare equipment), shared service providers (company providing services to several hospital systems), research laboratories and large, independent clinical laboratories, and depot repair service providers. BMETs also work for medical missionary type organizations such as International Aid, Medisend International and ORBIS (a flying eye hospital-DC10). The Army, Navy and Air Force also have trained biomedical equipment technicians.

BMET Employer Profile: Scott Sovocool

Scott Sovocool, director of biomedical engineering services for Methodist Health System, Dallas, handles three hospitals, five clinics—with two new specialty clinics being added—and supervises 22 techs. He spent 20 years in the military, in which he learned how to be a biomedical engineer. After earning his degree in business administration, he worked in the biomedical field at an imaging company and at hospitals in El Paso and Dallas. He's been with Methodist for 19 years.

Over those years, Sovocool has seen many changes, the biggest one in technology. Computerization has not only brought major changes in equipment, but it has also created higher demands on technicians. "It's gone from basic medical equipment to computerized equipment." Sovocool also recommended students learn networking and wireless systems. "Today, all of these huge computers are tied to medical records systems. They're tied to other systems that send information back and forth between them, so techs need to realize it's not just fixing a machine. You're fixing a machine, a computer and a network. The biomed of tomorrow is going to have to know networking, wireless computers and all of the latest technologies."

Thanks to ongoing training, a BMET doesn't have to know everything fresh out of college. Sovocool explained the hiring and placement process after graduation. "When BMETs come to us from TSTC, we put them in Biomed I positions. They can expect to be a Biomed I for about four years while they are trained on more and more advanced equipment. After four years, they're typically eligible to become a Biomed II, which runs for another four years. They move from basic equipment to monitoring equipment to defibrillators to ultrasound machines to anesthesia machines to OR lasers, and so on. After about eight years, then we have what we call the senior biomed position. And those techs are responsible for fixing chemical analyzers and very high tech equipment, very expensive, automated equipment."

When interviewing incoming BMETs, Sovocool looks beyond the expected high grades and recommendations. He also considers the attitude and passion of candidates. "When they come to talk to me, I want to know how well they communicate. I want to know if they have a strong positive attitude about their new job, what they're trying to get into and what they want to achieve. There's nothing worse than hiring an individual who doesn't want to be here. You need to have passion for patient care, passion for the job, and a desire to help the community and this hospital, because that's what we're all about. We're all about patients first."

One way to discern that passion, Sovocool suggested, is to look at what the student did outside of the classroom. "I think students need to be serious when they do their internships.

Before they get strongly committed into this field, they need to really know what it's all about. They need to go to the hospitals. If it's at all possible, they should go to a biomed engineering shop and spend some time. Some of our best technicians have turned out to be people who, long before they ever went to school, became volunteers within the medical atmosphere. They volunteered to work in a hospital or with community groups. This gives them a huge insight they didn't have before."

Troubleshooting CT Scanner

Necessary Skill Sets

Biomedical equipment technology is an evolving career field that requires skills, knowledge and abilities from both the technical environment and the healthcare environment. This rest of this chapter highlights the areas most critical to biomedical equipment technicians.

Electronics

Of all the electronics specialties, medical electronics has to be one of the most interesting. Medical transducers and sensors circuits take in signals received from the body, amplify them, filter them and transform them into meaningful measurements, which are used by physicians to make a diagnosis. Electronic circuits are also used to treat patients. For example, electrosurgical generators concentrate a large amount of high frequency energy into the tip of a scalpel-like blade to cut tissue and to stop bleeding during surgery. These are only a couple of the many uses of electronics in medical devices. In fact, all but the most basic of medical devices use electronic circuitry. In order to understand how this equipment operates, which is vital to the performance of their jobs, biomedical equipment technicians must have a thorough understanding of electronic theory and applications. They must also be proficient in using electronic test equipment such as oscilloscopes, digital multimeters, signal generators, frequency counters and spectrum analyzers. All of these skills are gained in biomedical equipment technology programs and internship.

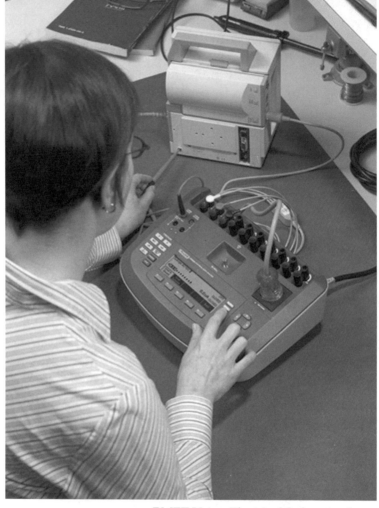

BMET Using Electrical Safety Analyzer

Anatomy & Physiology/Medical Terminology

How do medical devices interface with the human body? In order to know this, the BMET must know human anatomy and physiology and have a good grasp of medical terminology. Like any profession, healthcare has its own jargon and terminology and to understand the interface between man and machine, BMETs are obligated to know how each works. Of particular importance are the circulatory, respiratory, nervous and urinary systems.

BMET Employer Profile: Andrew Stiles

Andrew Stiles with Aramark, Inc., contracts with St. Joseph Regional Health Center in Bryan, Texas. He is director of clinical engineering services at the main facility, plus three rural access hospitals and 12 clinics. While earning a master's degree in healthcare administration, he gained experience across the country, from San Francisco to Boston and eventually back to Texas. He taught at TSTC and served on its BMET advisory board, and he was a board member at Angelina Community College in Lufkin, Texas.

While TSTC offers BMET students the opportunity to intern, Stiles said employers look to see whether the student took advantage of that opportunity, perhaps even going beyond the basic requirements. "If I looked at his resume, and I was trying to determine if he was proactive or not without speaking to him, I would look to see if he participated in the biomedical society, a regional one, whether it was in Houston or Dallas; whether he was in the BET club at TSTC; whether he volunteered time at an engineering department at a hospital, so he could truly get a picture that this was what he wanted to do in life."

After the BMET is hired, Stiles continues to expect the tech to be willing to learn on his own, take the initiative and, perhaps most importantly, not to have to be micromanaged. "If you have good proactive employees, they will set up their own goals and come to you. You end up getting thank you notes from the nurses or the department heads saying this is a wonderful person. That's how you know you have a valuable employee who you want to invest in and retain."

Stiles foresees continued job growth potential for BMETs. "There's always going to be a demand. If you're willing to take on new responsibilities that normally are not seen as part of the engineering department, the growth is whatever you allow it to be." But he knows firsthand that being part of the biomedical field means a lot of work and many hours. Despite that, when asked if he likes his job, Stiles quickly answers, "I love it. It's not very often that a person is aligned with his job. I like the diversity. I work with everybody—the plant operations, CEO, housekeepers."

Computers & Computer Networking

Forty years ago, computers and medical equipment would not likely have been mentioned in the same sentence. Today, computers are an integral part of the medical equipment industry in several ways. First, most complex monitoring, diagnostic and therapeutic medical equipment is microprocessor controlled. Some types of medical equipment actually look like computers, and in fact some are very close to being just that. There are devices that are nothing more than a specialized PC with a measurement module added, along with specific application software. For this reason, it is important for the biomedical equipment technician to have a solid knowledge base of computer hardware and be able to troubleshoot computer hardware.

BMETs also use several types of software. In addition to the Windows operating systems, some BMETs also work with other types of operating software such as UNIX and LINUX. BMETs also use a variety of application software. Technicians often use standard office application software such as Word, Excel and Access to create preventive maintenance procedures (based upon manufacturers' recommendations and other guidelines), write departmental memos, create databases of vendors and manufacturers and create spreadsheets for budgets and other applications. BMETs also use specialty software such as equipment management software that keeps track of medical equipment inventories, parts inventories, work orders, preventive maintenance and repair histories and many other functions. BMETs also use diagnostic software built into many complex medical devices such as diagnostic ultrasound machines, dialysis machines and patient monitors.

Computer networking skills are now considered critical for most biomedical equipment technicians. Modern intensive care units have patient monitors that measure heart rate, blood pressure, temperature and other vital signs in every room. These monitors are connected to each other to a central monitoring station and often to other patient monitors in other areas of the hospital. These monitors are networked so that a physician or nurse can retrieve one patient's vital signs or alarm status while standing in another patient's room. Also, most ultrasound machines, X-ray machines, computerized tomography systems (CT), nuclear medicine systems and MR units are connected to computerized radiography or digital radiography stations where the image is read by radiologists. The days of traditional X-ray film are just about over. Understanding how medical devices communicate over the network and how information flows is critical to troubleshooting and deciding if the network or the device is at fault.

BMETs use the Internet to look up parts, service information or locate other manufacturer or vendor information. BMETs may also use the Internet to communicate with other BMETs via list-servs such as the BIOMEDTALK listserv (http://bmetsonline. org). Many BMETs use the Internet for educational purposes, such as for furthering their formal education through online degree programs or taking other courses online.

Understanding wireless technology is also becoming important as some hospitals are moving toward wireless networks. Also, many hospitals are using RFID (Radio Frequency Identification) technology to track medical devices and patients.

Troubleshooting

Troubleshooting is a fundamental skill for biomedical equipment technicians. Troubleshooting is a logical process of looking for and locating a problem with a device. Troubleshooting skills get better with experience, of course, but BMETs need to a have a good problem solving mindset from the beginning. Learning the appropriate way to approach problems is a key component in becoming a successful troubleshooter.

BMETs perform many types of troubleshooting from connecting a digital multimeter to a power supply to determine if the voltage is correct to finding air leaks to measuring electromagnetic interference that might disrupt medical equipment operation. BMETs may perform very broad system-level troubleshooting to very specific, component-level troubleshooting depending on the device. They must be able to read schematics, wiring diagrams and flowcharts and be able to trace signals through a device to reach a faulty component, printed circuit board or module. They must be familiar with device-specific diagnostic software, sometimes used to make troubleshooting easier. BMETs must also be able to troubleshoot information flow from one device to another through a network and distinguish between device problems and network problems.

Operating X-ray Machine

Medical Equipment

BMETs must know how the equipment they maintain operates. In order to find out why a piece of equipment is not working, it is sometimes necessary for the BMET to interview the users of the equipment, such as physicians, nurses, respiratory therapists, radiology technicians and other allied healthcare personnel to determine how the equipment is supposed to function. However, most of the time, the BMET should already know how the equipment works. Most of this knowledge is gained in the BMET's education, on-the-job experience and from reading operator and service manuals.

Safety

BMETs must have a strong fundamental knowledge of safety in the healthcare environment. Biomedical equipment technology programs often spend a great deal of time covering electrical safety, biological safety, radiation safety and a variety of other safety issues common in the healthcare environment. BMETs also must know the different organizations concerned with healthcare safety such as the Joint Commission, OSHA and the FDA. As mentioned earlier, most hospital safety committees have at least one biomedical equipment technician as a member.

BMET Employer Profile: Ken Swartz

Ken Swartz was part of a development team at DuPont that invented and commercialized the first digital detector, the component that replaces X-ray film. Digital X-rays can be reviewed on monitors instead of printed to film, making hospitals film-less. Now manager of digital imaging support at Hologic, Inc., he is responsible for all technical support, managing the customer support center, the technical support center, and all technical training, including the apprentice program. Swartz is customer focused, which often means he travels a lot and sticks close to his Blackberry. "I live in Delaware and have an office in Boston and Delaware. Monday mornings I usually fly to Boston and fly back on Thursdays. I work in the Delaware office on Friday. I support other OEM companies that purchase products from us. So it's not unusual for me to be in China one week and Europe the next," Swartz says.

Swartz recommended that students working on their BMET degree try to get more hands-on experience by volunteering or working in a local hospital's biomed or med-imaging departments. He also values extra courses in networking. "In medical imaging, networking or connectivity is very important, since many hospitals have remote imaging centers that need to be networked in order for the radiologist to view and diagnose from another facility."

Swartz's apprentice program looks primarily at medical imaging students coming directly out of school with little experience. "We take them into our program and train them intensely on our complete product line. They work on the assembly floors; they attend our training programs and then travel around the country with other field engineers to gain on-the-job experience. After approximately nine months they graduate from the program and take over their own territory."

During this training period, Swartz also considers students' verbal and written communication skills. "Much of their job is, as we say, fixing the customer as well as fixing the equipment. They must be able to talk to hospital technicians, radiologists, etc., and also document on service records all they have done."

As a man who has been on the cutting edge of new developments in the biomedical imaging field, Swartz is well qualified to look into the future. He recognizes the demand for connectivity specialists. "The extensive knowledge of DICOM [Digital Imaging and Communications in Medicine] and networking is crucial, more so in the medical imaging arena. More remote facilities need to be connected." The demand for graduating BMETs and imaging techs is strong. "Hospitals will still be purchasing newer and more sophisticated equipment," Swartz said. "They are demanding faster response times so in some areas we are dedicating field engineers to their facility only. We have almost doubled our field engineering staff in the last year. I have more than doubled our customer support center staff and it is still growing."

Customer Service and People Skills

Of all the skills required of personnel in the medical equipment service industry, employers consistently rank customer service and "people" skills at the top of their list. The BMET's technical knowledge and ability are important, but the ability to effectively deal with people who are under stress will ultimately determine career success. The BMET must remember that when a medical device is "broken," the staff's ability to monitor, diagnose or treat the patient is hampered, therefore adding stress. For this reason, most of the calls for assistance the technician receives will be "emergencies." When multiple pieces of medical equipment need repair at the same time, the BMET may also begin to feel stressed. It is under these types of conditions when the BMET must be able to remain calm, assess the situation, set priorities and reassure staff that their problem will be corrected promptly. BMETs must treat each situation with professionalism and treat other members of the healthcare team with respect.

Prompt and professional service is only one aspect of effective customer service. Others include following up with the department after performing a repair to ensure customer satisfaction, returning phone calls and e-mails promptly and answering the telephone in a courteous and professional manner.

The ability to work as a team with co-workers is also important. Healthcare is a very diverse environment composed of professionals from many countries, cultures, religious beliefs, political beliefs, education levels, races and social backgrounds. Tolerance and respect are critical to performing well in this environment.

Troubleshooting X-ray Machine

Communication Skills

The healthcare industry is an educated industry; so as part of the healthcare team, biomedical equipment technicians must demonstrate excellent oral and written communication skills. BMETs regularly train hospital staff in the proper operation and safety of medical devices. This training may take place in front of a group or in one-on-one situations. BMETs also interface regularly with manufacturer sales and service representatives, department heads and hospital administration. The ability to speak clearly and effectively, without slang, cursing or other self-limiting mannerisms or gestures, can often influence credibility. Excellent writing skills are also necessary for documentation purposes and for writing reports. Documentation is a critical aspect of a BMET's job. Completed work orders, incident reports and other documentation can be used as legal documents in court.

Other Skills

In addition to the skills and knowledge mentioned previously, BMETs should also have good "shop skills." This means being able to identify and use the correct tool for the job. BMETs are also hardware experts. Medical devices are constructed with many types of fasteners and connectors. BMETs commonly replace coaxial cable connectors, electrical connectors, network connectors, power plugs, screws, nuts, bolts and a host of other specialty connectors and fasteners.

BMETs should also have good soldering skills. In most departments, BMETs only perform "through-hole" soldering and terminal connections when replacing components on printed circuit boards (although component level replacement is not nearly as common as it used to be, the skills to remove and solder common components are still necessary).

Although "professionalism" was covered under customer service skills, it also merits mention again under dressing professionally. Most BMETs no longer wear ties; however, many departments still require them, along with dress shirts and slacks. Most BMETs now have a business casual dress requirement with khaki pants or dress pants, polo type shirts or dress shirts and comfortable casual work shoes (not tennis shoes or flip-flops!). As a part of professionalism, BMETs should exhibit pride in workmanship and pay attention to detail. This means, for example, ensuring no screws or other fasteners are left out of a device after repair, the device is clean before being put back into service and settings for the device are returned to their pre-repair or performance check positions.

Time management is another skill that BMETs must acquire. Prioritizing work orders, preventive maintenance, training and administrative work is crucial to the career of the successful BMET. Many hospital biomedical engineering departments and independent service organizations are understaffed, and good time management skills are expected of BMETs to ensure the work gets completed and patient safety is not compromised.

Conclusion

The best thing that can happen in the operation of a hospital or clinic is for patients to take it for granted when the sophisticated medical equipment used does what it is supposed to do. When that happens, it's a safe bet that the doctors, nurses and other healthcare professionals who use that equipment don't take for granted the people who keep those machines operating properly. Those thousands of pieces of equipment are the tools of the trade in the medical profession.

Using PHANTOM to Test MRI

Repairing a Ventilator

Chapter 2: Biomedical Equipment Technician Education & Certification

When John Noblitt, Biomedical Equipment Technology instructor at Caldwell Community College and Technical Institute in Hudson, North Carolina, began his biomedical equipment technology career in 1985, technicians wore khaki work clothes and answered to management in the hospital maintenance division. "About 15 years ago, we dragged ourselves out of the basement and became a paraprofessional department, interacting with other hospital professionals, such as doctors and nurses," he says. What made the difference? Increasingly computerized and networked medical equipment required a new level of professionalism. Rather than dressing in khakis and carrying wrenches, today biomedical equipment technicians (BMETs) wear business casual clothing and carry laptops, along with the various tools required in the profession. Many hospitals now place BMET management in the IT (information technology) department.

As a result, teachers like Noblitt who have been in the field 10-20 years have seen an enormous amount of change. That change demands adaptability. Fifteen years ago, instructors taught component-level repairs, showing students how to find a malfunctioning component and repair or replace it only. Today's computerized circuit boards contain many small chips and solders, making it simpler and less expensive to replace the whole board, rather than attempting to replace a minute chip. As a result, BMET coursework across the country includes classes in computer networking and repair.

It follows, then, that students preparing for the field of biomedical equipment technology have a wide variety of courses ahead. Successful BMET students learn to speak the vernacular of the medical professional, dress appropriately for the job, cultivate strong people skills and develop critical thinking and problem solving strategies. Combine all of these abilities with computer networking, and an excellent candidate for a biomedical equipment technician emerges.

BMET Student Profile: Bradley Rushing

Second-year student Bradley Rushing had a background in electronics, but wanted something more.

"I wanted a new field, a job with stability, where I wasn't outside all the time," he says. "I'd always wondered who operated and maintained those big pieces of medical equipment."

When he was hospitalized for a short while, surrounded by the very machines he was curious about, he decided to look into a career in BMET. "A lot of people jump into school first and then choose the program," he says. "I chose the program first."

He moved from West Texas to attend Texas State Technical College Waco, the only school in the TSTC System that has on-site computerized tomography (CT) and magnetic resonance imaging (MRI) machines. It was also the only program with medical imaging technology.

He said his dream job would be to one day work as a field service representative. "When I was in the hospital, [the hospital staff] treated me so well," he says. "I find it so rewarding to be able to help people like they helped me."

Rushing said the most interesting experience he's had so far is a class in equipment safety and preventive maintenance. "It's the first time I actually got to put my hands on medical equipment," he says.

Rushing believes that having computer and mechanical skills before entering the program would benefit anyone interested in entering the field.

Educational Requirements

Most entry-level biomedical equipment technician and field service representative positions require an associate of applied science degree in biomedical equipment technology (or biomedical engineering technology or biomedical electronics technology) or military experience as a biomedical equipment technician. Currently, there are approximately 70 programs in the United States offering an associate of applied science degree in biomedical equipment (or engineering) technology (see http://www.iupui. edu/~cletcrse/webpages/bmet.html or www.aami.org for a complete list) or an associate of applied science degree in electronics technology with a specialization in biomedical electronics. Some four-year schools offer a bachelor's degree in biomedical engineering technology. Most two-year programs have courses in electronics, circuit analysis and troubleshooting, anatomy and physiology, medical terminology, biomedical instrumentation, computers and computer networking, healthcare safety and an internship in their curricula. The key to finding a successful BMET education program is to talk with faculty members, graduates of the program and employers of graduates.

BMET Instructor Profile: Thomas Dutton

TSTC Waco BMET instructor Tom Dutton believes that attitude provides the key to success. He works to instill integrity and honesty in the students who take his soldering and shop skills classes. "Most BMETs work alone," he says. "They must have the integrity to do the best work possible, even if no one is going to check their work." Dutton personalizes the point by asking students, "What if that piece of equipment had to save the life of someone you loved?" He insists that his BMETs not take short cuts. To prove his point, Dutton relates his own experience to his class. He has had several elective surgeries and with each ran a preventive maintenance (PM) check on all pieces of equipment to be used during his procedure. "Just because you have done PM on a piece of equipment for 10 years, and it has never failed, doesn't mean it won't fail next time," Dutton tells students.

He also stresses the need for adaptability. He says that besides being able to repair basic electronic equipment, students must have a working knowledge of fluid mechanics (hydraulics). They also need a familiarity with air dynamics, as would be the case with ventilators and some other life support equipment. Additionally, students need to know anatomy and physiology, as well as medical terminology. Finally, he tells students they must know computer networking and paperless systems.

Dutton comments that telemetry, or the mobility of a patient while connected to various monitors and pumps, is an increasing topic of concern in hospitals. Devices that measure telemetry connect to personnel and offices through wireless networks, and students must be able to effectively diagnose and repair any of these machines at whatever level they might malfunction. Dutton wants to be certain his students understand that in their everyday work life, they must apply the classroom knowledge they obtain. Because each situation is different, and there are so many types of equipment made by many manufacturers, they have to be able assimilate information quickly and look for other avenues of application. For instance, successful BMETs can translate repair information from one manufacturer's equipment to another of a similar type, even though not every component is the same. Dutton tells his students, "At the end of two years, you will have enough information to keep your head above water. You must be able to think and adapt."

The Two-Year Associate of Applied Science Degree

The associate of applied science degree was once considered a "terminal" degree and transferring credits into a four-year program was difficult, if not impossible. Today, many traditional colleges are offering "inverted" degrees in which an individual can transfer in a block of technical course credit (typically 36 hours) and common "core" academic courses (another 30 to 48 semester hours), and then take the upper level courses (approximately 42 to 60 semester hours) online, sometimes finishing the degree in as little as two years. These degrees often have names such as bachelor of applied technology, bachelor of applied science and technology or bachelor of applied management. They often capitalize on the technical background gained in the two-year degree and add leadership and management skills. These "inverted" degrees offer the fastest and least expensive track to a valuable four-year degree.

BMET Instructor Profile: Barbara Christe

Barbara Christe, Program Director for Biomedical Engineering Technology and Associate Director of Electrical Engineering Technology at Indiana University-Purdue University Indianapolis, entered the biomedical technology field 24 years ago. Though she had developed an interest in healthcare at an early age, she knew she did not want to be actively involved in patient care. Her aptitude for computers and electronics, combined with her medical interest, found a perfect home in BMET. Christe received her bachelor's degree in biomedical engineering and her master's degree in clinical engineering. After working two years at the University of Connecticut Health Center, she began teaching.

Like all of the instructors interviewed, Christe spoke at length about the connection between biomedical equipment technology and computers. "The task-oriented, VCR repairman approach is going away," she says. "The systems approach requires a higher level of thinking. Students must be able to understand how systems are connected and how they affect each other."

To clarify, Christe uses the example of a fetal monitor. All fetal monitors network to each other. Furthermore, they are networked to the nurse's station. A systems approach looks at what information these monitors transmit to each other and how they impact one another. Because this approach is so complex, more colleges and universities now offer bachelor's degrees in biomedical engineering. Students need to be aware that to work in this field, they must complete at least an associate's degree, but further education may help them obtain higher positions of responsibility.

Christe also emphasizes that BMET students must familiarize themselves with medical terminology. Many of the colleges teaching BMET require either anatomy and physiology or medical terminology. Some require both. The very nature of the profession requires interaction with medical staff, so students must be prepared with proper vocabulary and at least a cursory knowledge of the body systems and diseases.

The Four-Year Bachelor's Degree

For those aspiring to supervisory and management positions, a four-year degree is often necessary. The degree major is usually a matter of preference but business administration, healthcare management, information systems and engineering technology are all good choices. Ultimately, the choice will depend on the BMET's current degree, future plans, length of time the technician wishes to spend earning the degree and preference for face-to-face or online courses.

The key to pursuing any four-year degree is to verify that the institution is accredited by one of the six regional accrediting associations. Accreditation by one of these associations ensures maximum transferability to other colleges (such as a graduate school) and acceptance by employers. They are New England Association of Colleges and Schools (NEASC), North Central Association of Schools (NCA), Middle States Association of Schools and Colleges (MSA), Southern Association of Colleges and Schools (SACS), Western Association of Schools and Colleges (WASC), and the Northwest Commision on Colleges and Universities (NWCCU). Most colleges clearly state their accreditation by one of these six regional associations on their Web site. Claims to be licensed by a certain state or other claims to accreditation should be considered red flags and schools making these claims should be avoided.

BMET Student Profile: Letha Hargraves

"I want to be with my kids more," says Letha Hargraves, a first-year BMET student. "When I get my degree, I hope to work out of my home."

Hargraves worked as a hairdresser for 12 years, and found that while she really enjoyed working with people, she felt the need for a career change. She registered at TSTC, where she came across a pamphlet for BMET classes. She said she found the stability, benefits and pay of the BMET field appealing, and she decided to give it a shot. "I'm really excited about it," she says.

Looking ahead, Hargraves anticipates that her soldering and electronics classes will be her most challenging endeavor. But, she thinks that for some people, technical skills are easier to learn than people skills. "You need to at least have customer service skills, and a lot of patience," she says.

BMET Working at the Bench

Tuition & Fees

Many employers have tuition reimbursement to help defray the costs of obtaining a four-year degree. With many traditional colleges now offering courses online, working full time as a BMET and pursuing a four-year degree part time with an employer's assistance might ease the financial strain of more formal education. And, if the employer has a generous tuition benefit, the number of possibilities for online four-year programs is extensive. A good Web site to investigate accredited online programs is www. geteducated.com.

For those BMETs whose employers will not pick up the tab, there are still many economical options for obtaining a four-year degree from highly reputable universities. Many states have public universities with low tuition rates for in-state students. The University of North Texas has an inverted degree that accepts up to 85 semester credits toward a bachelor of applied arts and sciences in applied technology and performance improvement. The remaining 42 hours can be completed online (http://www.coe.unt.edu/LT/ATTD/degrees.php). (14 courses can be completed online for about $800 a course for in-state students.) The University of Texas at Brownsville has a bachelor of applied technology in computer information systems technology with a similar arrangement (http://bat.utb.edu/OAT/BAT.htm).

There are several schools with online inverted degree programs that charge the same tuition regardless of location. One example is the bachelor of applied science in management degree at Peru State College (PSC) in Peru, Nebraska. Up to 66 semester credit hours from the Associate of Applied Science Degree can be transferred into the program with the remaining hours (125 total) taken online at $157 a semester credit hour. More information on this degree program can be found at http://www.peru.edu/professionalstudies/programs/BASIntro.htm. Another example, the bachelor of science in technology studies in leadership, is offered by Fort Hays State University in Hays, Kansas, at $148 per semester credit hour and transfers 64 semester credit hours from an A.A.S. program (www.fhsu.edu/tecs/undergrad/index.shtml).

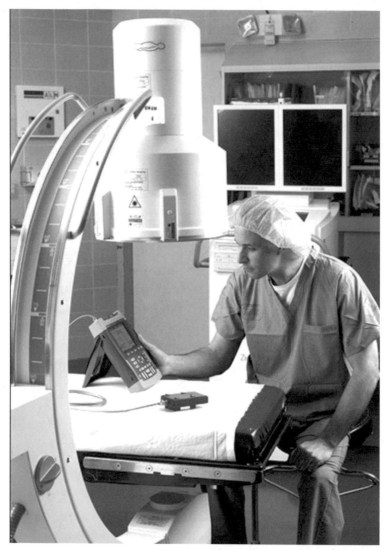

Testing a C Arm in Surgery

BMET Instructor Profile: John Noblitt

Like many others who come to the biomedical equipment technology field, John Noblitt of Caldwell Community College and Technical Institute wanted to work in the healthcare field without having to work directly with patients. The job stability provided by the BMET field, along with the opportunity to be part of a professional team of health providers, lured him to the profession 22 years ago. A natural teacher, being the son of two educators, Noblitt eventually left the active field to teach at the community college. His greatest satisfaction comes from helping struggling students master difficult concepts and then launching the new BMETs into their careers. As a teacher of medical instrumentation, he loves for students to ask questions and interact during class, so he can be sure they all gain a clear understanding of the equipment, techniques and thought processes involved.

Because of the high level of professionalism required in the BMET field, Noblitt emphasizes speaking the terminology of the hospital professional. Whether coming straight out of high school, with all the slang and casualness of teenagers, or changing careers mid-stride, BMET students face a learning curve when it comes to career vocabulary and demeanor. BMETs must develop soft skills, or interpersonal skills, and practice patience. Noblitt reminds his students often that they will have knowledge that other professionals do not. Just because the equipment operator knows how to use the machine does not mean that person understands the intricate workings of it. "Students must realize that medical professionals are concerned with things other than technology. This is a stressful, fast-paced job. Some of the problems you deal with may seem silly to you. But you must keep a patient perspective," he warns students.

In fact, being able to work well with others is so important in Noblitt's estimation that he labels lack of teamwork skills as being one of the main roadblocks to student success in the BMET field. He tells students they must have an overriding belief that they are part of a medical team. The BMET professional, however, is a behind-the-scenes person. While his work is of paramount importance to the whole system, it is mostly noticed only when something malfunctions. Therefore, Noblitt likes to leave students with this thought, "How good could an anesthesiologist be without a properly working machine? You are behind the scenes. You may not get kudos. Find your winning moments where you can and enjoy them."

BMET Certification

Certification for biomedical equipment technicians is usually voluntary, although some employers require certification. Three organizations offer a certification specifically for biomedical equipment technicians: the International Certification Commission (ICC) (www. aami.org), the Electronics Technician Association (www.etainternational.org), and the International Society of Certified Electronics Technicians (www. iscet.org).

Many entry-level BMETs ask why they should become certified if it is not required. Certification, while not required by all employers, shows an increased level of dedication and commitment to the field. It does not prove competence in a BMET, just as it does not prove competence in any other profession. What it does, however, is demonstrate motivation, initiative and an increased level of professionalism. Also, many employers pay certified BMETs more than non-certified BMETs, and many will pay the cost of becoming certified.

Operating X-ray machine

BMET Instructor Profile: Kenneth Tow

The first time TSTC Waco BMET instructor Kenneth Tow was called into an operating room to repair a piece of equipment, a patient lay on the table with his chest cut open. Many years later, Tow is teaching students to think on their feet and be prepared for anything. He relates the story of his operating room experience to illustrate how BMETs must be able to take stock of a situation and act quickly, without reacting to the unusual circumstances that might be around them. He likes to create life-like situations in his Introduction to Troubleshooting lab, and says, "If it *can* happen, it *will* happen."

Tow has been in the BMET field since 1976 and has seen innumerable changes. Critical thinking is the one skill requirement he says has remained constant throughout the years. The machines repaired by students in the classroom labs represent life and death situations in a hospital. The variety of electronic and computerized equipment in a healthcare facility is enormous, and Tow tells his students it is impossible to teach them how to repair every one. Instead, he teaches them how to apply the knowledge they gain in class. "I'm not here to teach you how to work on a specific piece of equipment," he tells them. "I'm here to teach you how to think." He works to build confidence in his students and wants to empower them with the ability to find answers on their own.

When asked what he sees as the biggest roadblock to student success, Tow replied, "Lack of motivation. If you just do your [classroom] time, get your grade and go home, you won't succeed." He asks students to consider how they would feel if they or someone they loved were in a life-threatening medical situation, and the tech working on their equipment had been a "C" student. Tow believes that while a "C" student may get hired initially, it's the "A" student who enjoys a long-lived and profitable career. Often, manufacturers or hospitals that require, and provide, further training for their employees hire BMET students. Tow says, "A students are normally more motivated and have better attitudes. Employers will be willing to invest in the student with a good attitude."

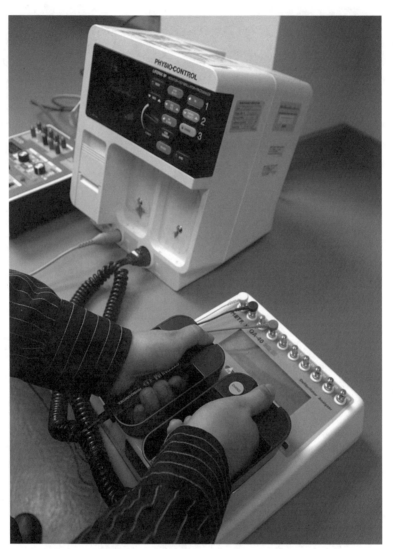

Testing Defibrillator with Defibrillator Analyzer

CBET Certification

The International Certification Commission's certification is by far the most recognized and the most widely held by biomedical equipment technicians. Over 6,000 people have been certified by the ICC as a Certified Biomedical Equipment Technician (CBET), a Certified Radiology Equipment Specialist (CRES), or a Certified Laboratory Equipment Specialist (CLES) since 1971. Currently, about 2,700 technicians hold active certifications with the ICC. Sometimes ICC certification is incorrectly referred to as AAMI certification. The Association for the Advancement of Medical Instrumentation serves as the secretariat for the ICC but does not issue the CBET, CRES or CLES certification.

To become a fully certified CBET, an applicant must meet *one* of the following eligibility requirements in addition to passing the exam:

- Associate degree in biomedical equipment technology and two years full-time BMET work experience; or

- Associate degree in electronics technology and three years full-time BMET work experience; or

- Four years full-time BMET work experience.

Applicants may also apply for "candidate status" if they do not meet all of the above requirements. Candidates are not fully certified until they meet the above requirements. However, the exam portion of the certification will be completed and the candidate has five years to complete the remaining work experience requirements. To take the exam as a candidate, applicants must meet at least one of the following requirements:

- Associate degree in biomedical equipment technology; or

- Associate degree in electronics technology and one year of full-time BMET work experience; or

- Completion of the U.S. military biomedical equipment technology program; or

- Two years of full-time BMET work experience.

A bachelor's degree does not substitute for work experience.

The CBET exam consists of 150 multiple choice questions taken from five categories: anatomy and physiology, safety in the healthcare facility, electricity and electronics, medical equipment function and operation and medical equipment problem solving. To pass the exam, an applicant must get 105 of the 150 questions correct. The exam costs $285 (as of 2008), and there is no limit to the number of times it may be taken. The ICC does not sponsor or endorse any study guide for the exam. However, an outline of exam content and list of reference material is provided in the applicant's exam handbook available online at the AAMI Web site. AAMI does sell a practice examination on CD that has proven very valuable for those who have taken the exam. Information on this CD titled *Assessing Your Knowledge* is also available on the AAMI Web site.

The requirements for CRES and CLES certification, also provided by the ICC, are the same as for the CBET certification with one exception. To become certified in either of these two specialty areas (radiology equipment or laboratory equipment), at least 40 percent of work experience over the last two years or 25 percent of work experience over the last five years must be in the designated specialty area. A person can still take the exam as a candidate with no experience, but to gain full certification, work experience requirements over the next two years must be in the specialty area.

Dialysis Certification for BMETs

Those BMETs specializing in dialysis equipment may choose to become Certified Biomedical Nephrology Technicians. This certification is offered by the National Nephrology Certification Organization. More information about this certification, along with the applicant handbook, can be found at http://www. ptcny.com/clients/NNCO/. This certification is for those BMETs working for dialysis centers and for manufacturers of dialysis equipment.

BMET Student Profile: Eric Brinkley

Eric Brinkley, a 40-year-old student in his second year of study, said he decided becoming a BMET would serve as a stepping stone to becoming an X-ray repair technician.

While Brinkley had previously worked at a hospital as a unit clerk and then an assistant unit manager, he still wanted to get his education. Fortunately, due to his wife's promotion, he was able to do so.

"I have five brothers with no education, and I want to set a good example for my kids and the rest of my family," he says. "One of my brothers works two jobs. I figure you can either have no education and work two bad jobs, or get an education and work one good job."

Brinkley believes that while technical skills can be learned, the ability to communicate effectively with others is necessary before training.

"When you don't understand something, you have to be able to speak up and not be embarrassed," Brinkley says. "Keep in mind that this medical equipment will be used on your mom, my mom, your grandmother . . . you just have to think about it like that."

Computer Certifications

Many BMETs are earning computer certifications, in addition to, or instead of, traditional biomedical certification. Most employers are now looking for thorough computer and computer networking knowledge and skills in entry-level BMET applicants. The A+ and Network + certifications offered by CompTIA are becoming more widespread and sought after evidence of this knowledge. The A+ certification is a vendor-neutral certification for personnel in computer support positions and is considered an entry-level certification. It covers computer support functions such as installation, configuration, troubleshooting, preventive maintenance and basic networking. It consists of two examinations, the first being the Essentials test and the second being one of three examinations: IT Technician, Remote Support Technician or Depot Technician. The Network + certification is more networking specific and consists of one 85 question multiple choice exam. Study guides for both the A+ and Network + exams are found in bookstores and through the CompTIA Web site (www.comptia.org). These computer certifications are not required; however, an entry-level BMET applicant having these on a resume would certainly have an edge over his or her competition.

CompTIA also offers a RFID + (Radio Frequency Identification) certification. With more and more hospitals using RFID technology, this is also a certification BMETs should consider.

Other computer certifications such as the Microsoft Certified Systems Engineer (MSCE) certification are also beneficial but not often obtained by entry-level BMETs. The MCSE is considered an advanced certification. For more information on this and other Microsoft certifications, see www.microsoft.com/trainingandservices.

BMET Instructor Profile: Dr. Roger Bowles

Dr. Roger Bowles, Program Director of Biomedical Equipment Technology at Texas State Technical College Waco, originally trained as a torpedo man on a nuclear submarine. Once he rejoined civilian life, Bowles began to investigate other careers. A family member introduced him to the idea of biomedical equipment repair. Being already familiar with TSTC, he got a catalog, looked up the courses and made a life-altering decision to study BMET in 1989. Through the years, Bowles has worked at Methodist Hospital in Dallas and at Reading Hospital and Medical Center in Reading, Pennsylvania. Along the way, he earned a master's degree in training and development and a doctorate in education. Ten years ago, Bowles became a teacher.

When asked what he enjoys most about teaching BMET, Dr. Bowles says, "I enjoy the field because I get a lot of satisfaction from it. I'm making a difference. By teaching, I can make a bigger impact. The more students I help to enter the field, the more patients I help."

In fact, Bowles currently oversees approximately 160 students in the BMET major at TSTC Waco. Regarding the success of the program, he says, "Because we began teaching BMET in the late 1960s, we are seen as an established program with a national reputation for producing excellent BMETs." Bowles also attributes TSTC's success to the fact that his entire current faculty worked in the profession before becoming teachers. "Our students learn from people who have been there and have first-hand experience in what the students will be doing upon graduation," he said. Additionally, the college houses a computerized tomography (CT) scanner and magnetic resonance imaging (MRI), providing hands-on experience with specialized equipment, an opportunity few other colleges around the nation can boast.

However, providing excellent equipment and hands-on repair experience alone does not ensure students will enjoy longevity as BMETs. Bowles feels that job success comes from having the appropriate motivation for the field. Although BMET can be a lucrative profession, he believes students should not enter the career for money alone. The satisfaction of a job well done and of knowing you are an integral part of a healthcare team should be the primary motivation for this career. Students must be able to function in a hospital environment, interacting with high-level professionals and conducting themselves in the same manner. "This field is 90 percent customer oriented," says Bowles, meaning that students who enter the field expecting to sit behind a workbench and repair equipment soon discover this is a people-oriented career. BMETs must cultivate the ability to function in a high stress facility and speak knowledgeably with medical staff to succeed. He emphasizes that students need to practice seeing themselves as healthcare professionals, even while still in the classroom.

To help students achieve the team mindset, he encourages them to read professional literature and become involved in the field from their first day in class. To cultivate a real world, rather than classroom, view of the career, he directs them to various professional organizations and publications. Some trade associations he recommends are:

- The North Texas Biomedical Association in Dallas, Texas (www.ntba.org)

- The Association for Advancement of Medical Instrumentation (www.AAMI.org)

- The Medical Equipment Technology Association (www.mymeta.org)

Dr. Bowles also recommends the following trade journals:

- *Health Imaging and IT Magazine* (www.healthimaging.com)

- *24x7* (www.24x7mag.com)

Testing Defibrillator Using Electrical Safety Analyzer &
Defibrillator Analyzer

Continuing Education

Medical technology is constantly evolving and the
biomedical equipment technician must keep up
with these changes to remain valuable to his or her
employer. BMETs read trade magazines and journals
such as *24 X 7* magazine (www.24x7mag.com),
Biomedical Instrumentation and Technology (www.aami.
org), *Medical Equipment Dealer* (www.mdpublishing.
com), *Health Imaging and IT* (www.healthimaging.
com), *The Journal of Clinical Engineering* and others to
find out the latest trends and happenings in the field.
There are also Web sites with information valuable to
BMETs such as www.dotmed.com.

Many BMETs also belong to regional and national
BMET associations. The regional associations usually
meet once every other month or once a quarter and
feature training on specific topics. These meetings
also provide an excellent avenue for networking with

peers and possible employers. Regional association yearly dues are usually very reasonable and many are under $30 a year. A list of regional associations can be found at www.aami.org and www.mymeta.org.

The Association for the Advancement of Medical Instrumentation (AAMI) is a national organization concerned with many areas of medical instrumentation, including device development, standards, research and, of course, service. Membership for full-time Biomedical Equipment Technology students is $30 a year and includes a subscription to the *Biomedical Instrumentation and Technology (BI&T)* journal. Membership for technicians with less than five years of experience is $100 a year. AAMI also has an annual conference featuring training on subjects of interest to BMETs and an exposition at which many manufacturers, independent service organizations, test equipment providers, recruiters and others meet and advertise their wares.

A newer national organization composed of BMETs was recently formed and is growing in numbers and in services. The Medical Equipment and Technology Association (www.mymeta.org) has dues of only $15 annually and provides ample opportunities for BMETs to become involved in their profession through various committees.

As mentioned in the Job Duties section in the previous chapter, most BMETs and field service representatives will attend manufacturer training on specific equipment through their employers. This training is usually one to four weeks in length, depending on the complexity of the equipment. For BMETs working at hospitals, the cost of this training is often worked into the purchase of the equipment.

Entry-level BMETs usually spend about six months to a year with their employer before being considered for manufacturers' training schools.

Conclusion

The instructors interviewed for this chapter have absorbed the changes in their careers and made the commitment necessary to help students move ahead in an ever-fluid environment. Each instructor profiled has more than 15 years of experience in his or her field, and though they teach a variety of classes in various colleges around the country, they all share two primary goals: the success of their students and the furthering of the biomedical equipment technology career as a whole.

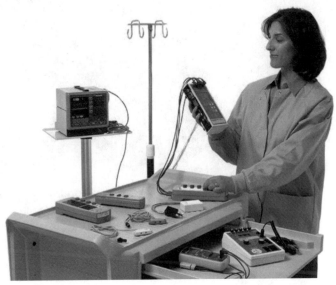

Testing a Patient Monitor

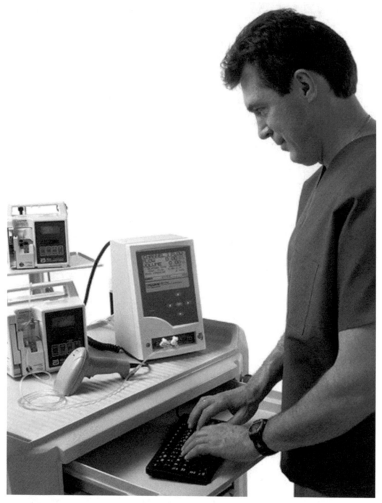

BMET Testing Infusion Pumps with Infusion Pump Analyzer

Chapter 3: Additional Biomedical Equipment Technician Information & Resources

Many people enter the BMET field as a way of helping others. Some claim the desire for job stability in addition to the satisfaction of lending a helping hand as their reasons for entering the field. According to a *24x7* survey, BMETs, in large part, comprise a happy and satisfied group of working Americans. In fact, the magazine said 91 percent of their readers would recommend the profession to others, because the overall feeling is that the profession offers a challenging, constantly-changing environment and a sense of value and importance among professionals. Most in the field say they wouldn't trade their job for anything, because they love helping people and they like who they work with. Not many other professions can say that.

BMET Higher Education Programs in the United States

Alabama

Jefferson State Community College
Birmingham, AL
Mr. Andy Hatley
ahatley@jeffstateonline.com
www.jscc.cc.al.us
205-856-8517
Certificate

Northwest-Shoals Community College
Muscle Shoals, AL
http://www.nwscc.cc.al.us
256-331-5200
Certificate

Arkansas

North Arkansas College
Harrison, AR
Mr. Ed Proctor
eproctor@northark.edu
http://www.northark.cc.ar.us/academics/bus_tech/
tech_votech/biomed.htm
870-391-3385
Associate of Applied Science Degree

Arizona

DeVry University
Phoenix, AZ
www.devry.edu/phoenix
602-870-9222
Bachelor's Degree

California

Los Angeles Valley College
Valley Glen, CA
Mr. Ronald Reis
www.lavc.cc.ca.us
818-947-2582
Associate Degree in Electronics with Biomedical
Electronics Option Certificate

DeVry University
www.devry.edu
Fremont, CA
510-574-1100
Pomona, CA
909-868-4240
Bachelor's Degree

Connecticut

Gateway Community College
North Haven, CT
Mr. Thomas McGrath
tmcgrath@gwcc.commnet.edu
http://www.gwcc.commnet.edu/academics.aspx
203-285-2378
Associate of Science Degree

Delaware

Delaware Technical and Community College
Terry Campus
Dover, DE
http://www.dtcc.edu/terry/pages/programs.htm
302-857-1000
Associate of Applied Science Degree in Electronics
with Biomedical Option

Florida

Broward Community College
North Campus
Coconut Creek, FL
Mr. John Rogers
jrogers@broward.edu
http://www.broward.edu
954-201-2292
Associate of Applied Science Degree

Florida Community College
Jacksonville, FL
Mr. Fred Wainwright
fwainwri@fccj.edu
www.fccj.edu
904-633-8100
Associate of Science Degree
Certificate

Santa Fe Community College
Gainesville, FL
Mr. Tom Mason
tom.mason@sfcc.edu
http://inst.sfcc.edu/~intech/electronics/
352-395-5362
Associate of Science Degree

DeVry University
www.devry.edu
Miramar, FL
954-499-9700
Orlando, FL
407-345-2800
Bachelor's Degree

Georgia

Central Georgia Technical College
Macon, GA
http://centralgatech.edu
478-757-3400
Certificate

Chattahoochee Technical College
Marietta, GA
Dr. Mike O'Rear
morear@chattcollege.com
www.chattcollege.com
770-528-4539
Associate of Applied Technology Degree

DeVry University
Decatur, GA
www.devry.edu
404-292-7900
Bachelor's Degree

Iowa

Southeastern Community College
West Burlington, IA
Mr. John Lenahan
jlenahan@scciowa.edu
http://www.secc.cc.ia.us
319-752-2731
Associate of Applied Science Degree in Electronics
with Biomedical Option

Western Iowa Tech Community College
Sioux City, IA
Mr. David McDonald
mcdonad@witcc.com
800-352-4649
Certificate

Illinois

South Suburban College
South Holland, IL
www.ssc.cc.il.us
708-596-2000
Associate of Applied Science Degree
Certificate

DeVry University
www.devry.edu
Addison, IL
630-953-1300
Chicago, IL
773-929-8500
Bachelor's Degree

Southern Illinois University – Carbondale
Carbondale, IL
Mr. Brian Kearney
bkearney@siu.edu
www.siu.edu
618-453-7219
Bachelor's Degree in Electronics Systems Technology
with a BMET Concentration

Indiana

Indiana University Purdue University at Indianapolis
Indianapolis, IN
Ms. Barbara Christe
Bchrist2@iupui.edu
www.iupui.edu
317-274-7591
Associate of Science Degree
Bachelor's Degree

Vincennes University
Vincennes, IN
Mr. Don Williams
dwilliams@vinu.edu
www.vinu.edu
812-888-5801
Associate of Applied Science Degree

Kentucky

Madisonville Community College
Madisonville, KY
Mr. Joey Jones
www.madcc.kctcs.net
270-824-7544
Associate of Applied Science Degree

Louisiana

Delgado Community College
New Orleans, LA
Mr. George Platt
gplatt@dcc.edu
www.dcc.edu
504-671-6190
Associate of Applied Science Degree in Electronics
Servicing Technology with Biomedical Equipment
Repair Option

Louisiana Technical College
Sullivan Campus
Bogalusa, LA
www.ltc.edu
985-732-6640
Associate of Applied Science Degree
Certificate

Maryland

Howard Community College
Columbia, MD
Mr. Daniel Friedman
dfriedman@howardcc.edu
www.howardcc.edu
410-772-4827
Associate of Applied Science Degree Certificate

Massachusetts

Benjamin Franklin Institute of Technology
Boston, MA
www.bfit.edu
617-423-4630
Associate in Engineering Degree

Quinsigamond Community College
Worcester, MA
Mr. James Heffernan
jheffernan@qcc.mass.edu
www.qcc.mass.edu
508-854-2739
Associate in Science Degree

Michigan

Schoolcraft College
Livonia, MI
Mr. Chris Peters
cpeters@schoolcraft.edu
www.schoolcraft.cc.mi.us
734-462-4400 x 5162
Associate of Applied Science Degree

Minnesota

Anoka-Ramsey Community College
Coon Rapids, MN
http://www.anokaramsey.mnscu.edu/
763-422-3333
Associate in Science Degree

Dakota County Technical College
Rosemount, MN
Mr. Steven Bezanson
Steve.Bezanson@dctc.edu
www.dctc.edu
651-423-8378
Associate of Applied Science Degree

Missouri

Linn State Technical College
Linn, MO
Mr. Vince Geiger
vince.geiger@linnstate.edu
www.linnstate.edu
573-897-5226
Associate of Applied Science Degree in Electronics
Engineering Technology – Biomedical Engineering
Technology Option

St. Louis Community College
Florissant Valley
St. Louis, MO
http://www.stlcc.edu/fv/
314-595-4308
Associate of Applied Science Degree in Electronic
Engineering Technology – Biomedical Engineering
Technology Option

DeVry University
Kansas City, MO
www.devry.edu
816-941-0430
Bachelor's Degree

New Jersey

County College of Morris
Randolph, NJ
www.ccm.edu
973-328-5000
Associate of Applied Science Degree

Thomas Edison State College
Trenton, NJ
www.tesc.edu
888-442-8372
Associate of Science in Applied Science and
Technology
Bachelor of Science in Applied Science and
Technology

DeVry University
North Brunswick, NJ
www.devry.edu
732-435-4880
Bachelor's Degree

New Jersey Institute of Technology
Newark, NJ
Mr. William Barnes
barnesw@adm.njit.edu
www.njit.edu
973-596-3228
Bachelor of Science in Electrical and Computer
Engineering Technology with Biomedical
Specialization

New Mexico

Dona Ana Community College
Las Cruces, NM
Mr. Oscar Perez
operez@nmsu.edu
http://dabcc-www.nmsu.edu/
505-527-7586
Associate of Applied Science Degree

New Mexico State University at Alamogordo
Alamogordo, NM
Mr. Steve Holmes
sholmes1@charter.net
http://alamo.nmsu.edu/
505-439-3690
Associate of Applied Science Degree

New York

DeVry University
Long Island City, NY
www.devry.edu
718-472-272
Bachelor's Degree

North Carolina

Caldwell Community College and Technical Institute
Hudson, NC
Mr. John Noblitt
jnoblitt@cccti.edu
http://www.caldwell.cc.nc.us/
828-726-2200
Associate of Applied Science Degree

Stanley Community College
Albemarle, NC
Mr. Dave Wilson
wilsonwd@stanly.cc.nc.us
www.stanly.cc.nc.us
704-991-0277
Associate of Applied Science Degree

Ohio

Cincinnati State Technical and Community College
Cincinnati, OH
Mr. Steve Yelton
Steven.yelton@cincinnatistate.edu
http://www.cinstate.cc.oh.us/
513-569-1500
Associate of Applied Science Degree

Cuyahoga Community College
Cleveland, OH
www.tri-c.edu
800-954-8742
Associate of Applied Science Degree in Electrical/
Electronics Engineering Technology with Biomedical
Concentration

Owens Community College
Toledo, OH
Mr. Paul Svatik
paul_svatik@owens.edu
www.owens.edu
419-661-7000
Associate of Applied Science Degree with
Biomedical Electronics Major Certificate

DeVry University
Columbus, OH
www.devry.edu
614-253-7291
Bachelor's Degree

Oklahoma

Tulsa Community College
Tulsa, OK
Mr. Thomas Henderson
thenders@tulsacc.edu
www.tulsacc.edu
918-595-7492
Associate of Applied Science Degree

Oregon

Portland Community College
Portland, OR
www.pcc.edu
503-977-4163
Associate of Applied Science Degree in Electronic
Engineering Technology with Biomedical Engineering
Technology Major

Pennsylvania

Erie Institute of Technology
Erie, PA
www.erieit.edu
814-868-9900
Associate of Specialized Technology (not regionally
accredited)

Johnson College
Scranton, PA
Mr. Doug Hampton
dhampton@johnson.edu
www.johnsoncollege.edu
570-342-6404
Associate in Applied Science Degree (not regionally accredited)

Pennsylvania State University – New Kensington
New Kensington, PA
Mr. Myron Hartman
Mdh15@psu.edu
http://www.nk.psu.edu/
724-334-6712
Associate in Engineering Technology

DeVry University
Fort Washington, PA
www.devry.edu
215-591-5700
Bachelor's Degree

South Carolina

York Technical College
Rock Hill, SC
www.yorktech.com
803-327-8008
Certificate

South Dakota

Southeast Technical Institute
Sioux Falls, SD
Mr. Paul Syverson
paul.syverson@southeasttech.com
www.southeasttech.com
605-367-5512
Associate of Applied Science Degree

Tennessee

East Tennessee State University
Johnson City, TN
Mr. Hugh Blanton
blanton@etsu.edu
www.etsu.edu
423-439-4177
Bachelor of Science Degree in Biomedical Engineering
Technology

Texas

Houston Community College
Houston, TX
www.hccs.edu
713-718-5117
Associate of Applied Science Degree in Electronic
Engineering Technology – Biomedical Electronics
Specialization

St. Philip's College
San Antonio, TX
Mr. Richard Lundquist
rlundqui@accd.edu
www.accd.edu
210-531-3414
Associate of Applied Science Degree

Texas State Technical College Harlingen
Harlingen, TX
www.harlingen.tstc.edu
956-364-4851

Texas State Technical College Marshall
Marshall, TX
Mr. Wilson Jones
Wilson.Jones@marshall.tstc.edu
www.marshall.tstc.edu
903-923-3364
Associate of Applied Science Degree

Texas State Technical College Waco
Waco, TX
Dr. Roger Bowles
Roger.Bowles@tstc.edu
www.waco.tstc.edu/bet
254-867-2669
Associate of Applied Science Degree

DeVry University
www.devry.edu
Houston, TX
713-973-3000
Irving, TX
972-929-6777
Bachelor's Degree

Utah

Salt Lake Community College
Salt Lake City, UT
www.slcc.edu
801-957-3274
Associate of Applied Science Degree in Electronics
Technology with Biomedical Emphasis

Virginia

ECPI College of Technology
Virginia Beach, VA
Mr. Loren Tracy
Ltracey@ecpi.edu
www.ecpi.edu
757-671-7171
Associate of Applied Science Degree

Washington

Bates Technical College
Tacoma, WA
Mr. Art Cutting
acutting@bates.ctc.edu
www.bates.ctc.edu
253-680-7252
Associate of Technology Degree

Bellingham Technical College
Bellingham, WA
www.btc.ctc.edu
360-752-7000
Associate of Applied Science Degree in Electronics
with Biomedical Equipment Option

North Seattle Community College
Seattle, WA
Ms. Lynda Wilkinson
lwilkins@sccd.ctc.edu
www.sccd.ctc.edu
206-528-4588
Associate of Applied Science Degree

Spokane Community College
Spokane, WA
Mr. Chris Coelho
ccoelho@scc.spokane.edu
www.scc.spokane.edu
509-533-7299
Associate of Applied Science Degree

DeVry University
Federal Way, WA
www.devry.edu
253-943-2800
Bachelor's Degree

Wisconsin

Milwaukee Area Technical College
Milwaukee, WI
http://www.milwaukee.tec.wi.us/
414-297-6000
Associate of Applied Science Degree

Western Wisconsin Technical College
La Crosse, WI
Mr. Fred Dorau
dorauf@wwtc.edu
800-248-9982
Associate of Applied Science Degree

BMET Two- and Four-Year Degree Plans

Biomedical Equipment Technology and Medical Imaging Systems Technology Degree Programs at Texas State Technical College Waco

The Biomedical Equipment Technology (BET) program at Texas State Technical College Waco is one of the oldest two-year programs in the United States and one of the largest, with more than 160 students currently enrolled. The BET program at TSTC Waco has been producing quality entry-level biomedical equipment technicians for over three decades and has graduates working throughout Texas and much of the United States. Six full-time faculty combine more than 80 years of actual BMET experience and more than 40 years of teaching experience in the biomedical equipment technology field. The program has a large inventory of operational medical equipment including defibrillators, ventilators, patient monitors, blood gas analyzers, infusion pumps, diagnostic ultrasound machines, X-ray machines and portable X-ray machines, a CT unit and an MRI. The program also maintains the latest in biomedical test equipment.

The Biomedical Equipment Technology Program at TSTC Waco is six semesters, including one semester of cooperative education or internship, and takes approximately two years to complete for a full-time student (students complete three full semesters per year including the summer semester). Courses are lab-oriented and offer maximum opportunity for hands-on experience with actual medical equipment. Hospital employers (in-house) of the BET program include Methodist Medical Center in Dallas, Baylor

Medical Center in Dallas, Hillcrest Baptist Medical Center in Waco and VA Medical Center in Temple. ISO employers of graduates include Aramark, Masterplan, GE Healthcare, Healthcare Biomedical Services, Crest Services, South Plains Biomedical and Universal Hospital Services. Manufacturer employers include Fresenius Medical Care North America (also operates dialysis centers), Spacelabs Medical and HealthTronics.

The program at TSTC Waco also offers the Medical Imaging Systems Technology degree program. The MIT program is similar to the BET program in the first few semesters but the last semester focuses on diagnostic imaging systems, such as advanced X-ray and CT, instead of general medical equipment and clinical laboratory equipment. Hospital employers of the MIT program include Methodist Medical Center of Dallas and Methodist Charlton Medical Center. ISO employers include Masterplan, Aramark and Medical Equipment Services of Denton. Manufacturer employers include Hologic, GE Medical Systems and Siemens Medical Systems.

An outline of both the BET and MIT programs is included below:

Students Starting Fall 05

Effective 9/1/08		Texas State Technical College Waco		FICE Code: 003634	
Students Starting	Fall 2008	Biomedical Equipment Technology		HEGIS Code: 8421	
				CIP Code: 15.0401	
First Semester			Lec	Lab	Cr	CH
ENGL 1301		Composition I **Prerequisite: None**	3	0	3	48

MATH 1332 or MATH 1314	College Math/College Algebra **Prerequisite: None**	3	0	3	48
IEIR 1371	DC/AC Electronics **Prerequisite: DMTH 0050**	1	7	3	128
BIOM 1101	Biomedical Equipment Technology **Prerequisite: None**	1	0	1	16
ITSC 1325	Personal Computer Hardware **Prerequisite: READ 0200**	2	4	3	96
BIOM 1205	Soldering Skills & Shop Safety **Prerequisite: None**	0	6	2	96
	TOTALS	**10**	**17**	**15**	**432**
Second Semester					
PSYC 2301 or SOCI 1301	General Psyc. or Introductory Sociology **Prerequisite: None**	3	0	3	48
HUMA 1301 or approved elective	Humanities **Prerequisite: ENGL 1301**	3	0	3	48
CETT 1325	Digital Fundamentals **Prerequisite: IEIR 1371**	1	8	3	144
BIOM 1309	Applied Biomedical Equipment Technology **Prerequisite: None**	2	4	3	96
ITNW 1325** ** or ITNW 1358	Fundamentals of Networking **Prerequisite: ITSC 1325**	2	4	3	96
	TOTALS	**11**	**16**	**15**	**432**
Third Semester					
CHEM 1305 or approved elective	Introductory Chemistry I	3	0	3	48
BIOM 1341	Medical Circuits/Troubleshooting **Prerequisite: IEIR 1371**	2	4	3	96
BIOM 2301	Safety in Healthcare Facilities **Corequisite: IEIR 1371**	1	4	3	80
BIOM 2341	General Medical Equipment I **Corequisite: IEIR 1371**	2	4	3	96
	TOTALS	**8**	**12**	**12**	**320**
Fourth Semester					
BIOM 1350	Diagnostic Ultrasound Imaging System **Corequisite: IEIR 1371**	2	4	3	96
BIOM 2335	Physiological Instruments I **Prerequisite: 2341- IEIR 1371**	2	4	3	96
BIOM 1315	Medical Equipment Networks **Prerequisite: ITNW 1325 or 1358**	2	4	3	96
BIOM 2349	Basic X-Ray & Medical Imaging Systems **Prerequisite: IEIR 1371**	1	4	3	80
	TOTALS	**7**	**16**	**12**	**368**
Fifth Semester					
BIOM 2331	(Clinical) Instrumentation **Prerequisite: BIOM 2301**	2	4	3	96
BIOM 2339	Physiological Instruments II **Prerequisite: BIOM 2301**	2	4	3	96
BIOM 2343	General Med. Equipment II **Prerequisites: BIOM 2341, 2301, IEIR 1371**	2	4	3	96
BIOM 2357	Biomed Equip. Tech. Prof. Review **Prerequisite: BIOM 2301**	2	4	3	96
	TOTALS	**8**	**16**	**12**	**384**
Sixth Semester					
*BIOM 2680	Cooperative Education - Biomed Tech **Prerequisite: BIOM 2301**	1	39	6	640
	TOTALS	**45**	**104**	**72**	**2576**

			Lec	Lab	Cr	CH
OR						
BIOM 2388		Internship - Biomedical Tech **Prerequisite: BIOM 2301**	0	9	3	144
BIOM 2389		Internship - Biomedical Tech **Prerequisite: BIOM 2301**	0	9	3	144
OR						
BIOM 2380		Cooperative Education - Biomed Tech **Prerequisite: BIOM 2301**	1	19	3	320
BIOM 2381		Cooperative Education - Biomed Tech **Prerequisite: BIOM 2301**	1	19	3	320
*CAPSTONE COURSE						

Students Starting Fall 05

Effective 9/1/08		Texas State Technical College Waco		FICE Code: 003634		
Students Starting	Fall 2008	Medical Imaging Systems Technology		HEGIS Code: 8421		
				CIP Code: 15.0401		
First Semester			Lec	Lab	Cr	CH
ENGL 1301		Composition I	3	0	3	48
MATH 1332 or MATH 1314		College Math/College Algebra	3	0	3	48
IEIR 1371		DC/AC Electronics **Prerequisite: DMTH 0050**	1	7	3	128
BIOM 1101		Biomedical Equipment Technology **Prerequisite: None**	1	0	1	16
ITSC 1325		Personal Computer Hardware **Prerequisite: READ 0200**	2	4	3	96
BIOM 1205		Soldering Skills & Shop Safety **Prerequisite: None**	0	6	2	96
		TOTALS	**10**	**17**	**15**	**432**
Second Semester						
PSYC 2301 or SOCI 1301		General Psyc. or Introductory Sociology	3	0	3	48
HUMA 1301/or approved elective		Humanities **Prerequisite: ENGL 1301**	3	0	3	48
CETT 1325		Digital Fundamentals **Prerequisite: IEIR 1371**	1	8	3	144
BIOM 1309		Applied Biomedical Equipment Technology **Prerequisite: None**	2	4	3	96
ITNW 1325**		Fundamentals of Networking **Prerequisite: ITSC 1325**	2	4	3	96
** or ITNW 1358		**TOTALS**	**11**	**16**	**15**	**432**
Third Semester						
CHEM 1305/or approved elective		Introductory Chemistry I	3	0	3	48
BIOM 1341		Medical Circuits/Troubleshooting **Prerequisite: IEIR 1371**	2	4	3	96
BIOM 2301		Safety in Healthcare Facilities **Corequisite: IEIR 1371**	1	4	3	80

BIOM 2341		General Medical Equipment I **Corequisite: IEIR 1371**	2	4	3	96
		TOTALS	**8**	**12**	**12**	**320**
Fourth Semester						
BIOM 1350		Diagnostic Ultrasound Imaging System **Corequisite: IEIR1371**	2	4	3	96
BIOM 2335		Physiological Instruments I **Prerequisite: 2341- IEIR 1371**	2	4	3	96
BIOM 1315		Medical Equipment Networks **Prerequisite: ITNW 1325 or 1358**	2	4	3	96
BIOM 2349		Basic X-Ray & Medical Imaging Systems **Prerequisite: IEIR 1371**	1	4	3	80
		TOTALS	**7**	**16**	**12**	**368**
Fifth Semester						
BIOM 2447		R/F X-Ray Systems **Prerequisite: BIOM 2349**	2	4	4	96
BIOM 2433		Digital Radiography **Prerequisite: BIOM 2349**	2	4	4	96
BIOM 2445		Advanced Imaging Systems **Prerequisite: BIOM 2349**	2	4	4	96
		TOTALS	**6**	**12**	**12**	**288**
Sixth Semester						
*BIOM 2680		Cooperative Education - Biomed Tech - **Prerequisite: BIOM 2301**	1	39	6	640
		TOTALS	**43**	**100**	**72**	**2480**
OR						
BIOM 2388		Internship - Biomedical Tech. - **Prerequisite: BIOM 2301**	0	9	3	144
BIOM 2389		Internship - Biomedical Tech. - **Prerequisite: BIOM 2301**	0	9	3	144
OR						
BIOM 2380		Cooperative Education-Biomedical Tech- **Prerequisite: BIOM 2301**	1	19	3	320
BIOM 2381		Cooperative Education-Biomedical Tech- **Prerequisite: BIOM 2301**	1	19	3	320
*CAPSTONE COURSE						

The Biomedical Equipment Technology program also is offered at Texas State Technical College Harlingen and Texas State Technical College Marshall.

Biomedical Equipment Technology Two-Year Degree Program at Caldwell Community College and Technical Institute (Hudson, NC)

The BET program prepares individuals to install, operate, troubleshoot and repair sophisticated devices and instrumentation used in the healthcare delivery system. Emphasis is placed on preventive and safety inspections to ensure biomedical equipment meets local and national safety standards.

The coursework in the program provides a strong foundation in mathematics, physics, electronics, anatomy and physiology and troubleshooting techniques. Some courses will include job experience and job shadowing, as well as people skills and communication, both in written and oral form.

Fall Semester I	
BMT 111	Introduction to Biomed Field
CIS 113	Computer Basics
MAT 121	Algebra/Trig.
ELC 112	DC/AC Electricity
NET 125	Networking Basics
Elective	Humanities and Fine Art
Spring Semester I	
COM 120	Interpersonal Communications
ELN 131	Electronic Devices
ELN 133	Digital Electronics
PHY 131	Physics – Mechanics
NET 126	Routing Basics
Summer Semester I	
ENG 111	Expository Writing

BMT 120	Biomedical Anatomy & Physiology
BMT 112	Hospital Safety & Standards
Fall Semester II	
SEC 110	Security Concepts
BMT 212	BMET Instrumentation I
ENG 114	Professional Research & Reporting
BMT 223	Imaging Technology/Laser Fundamentals
NET 175	Wireless Technology
Spring Semester II	
BMET 213	BMET Instrumentation II
BMT 225	Biomedical Troubleshooting
COE 115	Work Experience Seminar
COE 112	Co-op Work Experience I
Elective	Social Science
A.A.S. Degree	**Total Credit Hours: 76**

Graduates should qualify for employment opportunities in hospitals, clinics, clinical laboratories, shared service organizations and manufacturers' field service. With an A.A.S. degree and two years of experience, individuals should be able to become a certified Biomedical Equipment Technician.

Biomedical Engineering Technology Two- and Four-Year Degree Program at Indiana University Purdue University Indianapolis

IUPUI (a campus of Purdue University and Indiana University) offers a bachelor's degree (B.S.) in Biomedical Engineering Technology. The degree has a focus on the practice of medical equipment support in the clinical environment. The degree can build on a person's associate's degree and many courses are available at a distance.

Purdue University is one of the few schools in
the country to offer coursework which leads to
a bachelor's degree in Biomedical Engineering
Technology (with a clinical focus). This curriculum
is not designed to prepare graduates for work in
research, to attend medical school or other typical
"Biomedical Engineering" career paths. For BMETs
already in the field, the program might have been
called clinical engineering or biomedical equipment
technology.

Many of the courses are delivered in the virtual
Internet classroom, called Oncourse, without concern
for a student's geographic location. The courses
follow a typical 15-week college semester and are not
"independent study."

The B.S. program has been made possible with a
financial contribution from the Aramark Corporation.
These funds allow IUPUI to develop the online
courses which focus on BMET content.

1st Semester			
Course #	Units	Title	Pre- or Co-requisite
BMET 105	1	Intro to BMET	
TECH 102	1	Discovering Technology	
TECH 105	3	Intro to Engr Tech	
ECET 109	3	Digital Fundamentals	P or C: MATH 111 or instructor's consent
MATH 153	3	Algebra & Trigonometry I	P: MATH 111
ENGL W131	3	Elementary Composition	Placement
TOTAL	14		

2nd Semester			
Course #	Units	Title	Pre- or Co-requisite
ECET 107	4	Introduction to Circuit Analysis	MATH 602 placement test of 45 or above
ECET 155	3	Digital Fundamentals II	P: ECET 109
MATH 154	3	Algebra & Trigonometry II	P: MATH 153
COMM R110	3	Fund of Speech Communication	
BMET 220	3	Applied Human Biology for BMET	
TOTAL	**16**		

3rd Semester			
Course #	Units	Title	Pre- or Co-requisite
BMET 209	2	BMET Microprocessor Applications	P: ECET 109
BMET 240	3	Intro to Medical Electronics	P: BMET 220 & knowledge of electronics
PHYS 218	4	General Physics	P: MATH 159 or equiv.
ECET 157	4	Electronics Circuit Analysis	P: ECET 107 & MATH 153
MATH 221	3	Calculus for Tech I	P: MATH 159 or MATH 154
TOTAL	**16**		

4th Semester			
Course #	Units	Title	Pre- or Co-requisite
BMET 320	4	Biomedical Electronics Systems	P: BMET 240 and ECET 157
BMET 290	4	DMET Practicum	P or C: BMET 320
ECET 207	4	AC Electronics Circuit Analysis	P or C: ECET 157 & MATH 154

Course #	Units	Title	Pre- or Co-requisite
ECET 234	3	PC Systems I	P: ECET 109
PSY B104	3	Psychology as a Social Science	
TOTAL	18		
	64	Total Credit Hours A.S. Degree	

5th Semester

Course #	Units	Title	Pre- or Co-requisite
IET 150	3	Quantitative Methods for Tech	P: MATH 159
BMET 310	3	Intro to Radiography Systems	P: BMET 220 or equiv.
MATH 222	3	Calculus for Technology II	P: MATH 221
BUS A200	3	Accounting	P: Sophomore standing
TCM 220	3	Technical Report Writing	P: ENGL W131 or equiv.
TOTAL	**15**		

6th Semester

Course #	Units	Title	Pre- or Co-requisite
BMET 420	3	Techn & Special Patient Populations	P: BMET 320 or equiv.
CHSS Elec	3	See approved course list	
ECET 284	4	Computer Communications	P: ECET 155 and ECET 157
TCM	3	Written Comm for Sci & Industry	P: ENGL W131 & junior standing
CHSS Elec	3	See approved course list	
TOTAL	**16**		

7th Semester			
Course #	**Units**	**Title**	**Pre- or Co-requisite**
BMET 440	3	Codes Reg & Patient Safety	P: BMET 320 or equiv.
ECET 490	1	Senior Design Project Phase I	P: Three ECET 300 or 400 level ECET Elec
ECET 493	1	Ethics & Professionalism in Tech	
CHEM C110	3	The Chemistry of Life LED	
CHEM C115	2	The Chemistry of Life LAB	P or C: CHEM C110
NURS B231	3	Comm for the Health Care Prof.	
ECET 483	4	Networking Fund w/ Microcontrollers	P: ECET 234, ECET 284
TOTAL	**17**		

8th Semester			
Course #	**Units**	**Title**	**Pre- or Co-requisite**
BMET 470	3	Special Topics in BMET	P: CHEM 110 & BMET 320 or equiv.
BMET 491	2	Technical Project	P: 3 BMET 300 or 400 level courses & ECET 490
OLS Elec	3	See approved course list	
OLS Elec	3	See approved course list	
CHSS Elec	3	See approved course list	
TOTAL	**14**		
	126	**Total Credit Hours B.S. Degree**	

The B.S. degree requires 41 courses. The distance education portion of the degree is the junior and senior level coursework, designed to build on previous study or experience. Many of the freshman and sophomore level classes (the first twenty courses) are electrical in nature and may require on-campus work. Freshman and sophomore level students not able to attend classes in Indianapolis can work with an advisor to seek another school (with matching accreditation) at which to take the classes and transfer them to IUPUI. For freshman and sophomore level students, this may not be an easy or convenient process. In addition, students may be limited by the offerings at schools which are geographically close to them.

While some courses are available through distance education, most educators agree that some subjects, chemistry for example, are best learned in a traditional classroom setting. The program has been designed to allow almost all junior and senior level courses to be available over a distance. Junior and senior level courses which are not offered over a distance are widely available at most institutions of higher education. Students who are unable to come to Indianapolis will be encouraged to seek courses not available via the Internet from local schools with appropriate accreditation. For students with no BMET or electronics background or work experience, this may not be an easy or convenient process.

BMET Employers, Equipment Manufacturers & Recruiters

Independent Service Organizations (ISOs)

Aramark
www.aramark.com

Crest Services
www.crestservices.com

GE Healthcare
www.gehealthcare.com

Kinetic Biomedical
www.kineticbiomedical.com

Legacy Biomedical
www.legacybiomedical.com

Masterplan
www.masterplan-inc.com

Medical and Scientific Repair Services (MERA)
www.meraserv.com

Modern Biomedical and Imaging
www.modernbiomedical.com

Penn Biomedical Support
www.pennbiomed.com

Reliance Biomedical
www.reliancebiomed.com

Sodexho
www.sodexho.com

South Plains Biomedical
www.spbs.com

Technology in Medicine
www.techmed.com

Trimedx
www.trimedx.com

Universal Hospital Services
www.uhs.com

In-House Biomedical/Clinical Engineering Departments

Duke University Health System
clinicalengineering.duhs.duke.edu/

Flinders University Australia
som.flinders.edu.au/FUSA/BME/Clin/ClinGrp.htm

University of Arkansas for Medical Sciences
www.uams.edu/ClinEng/default.aspx

University of Virginia Health System
www.healthsystem.virginia.edu/internet/clinical-eng/

Wake Forest University Baptist Medical Center
www1.wfubmc.edu/cem/

Medical Equipment Manufacturers

Accuray
www.accuray.com
robotic radiosurgery

Baxter Healthcare
www.baxter.com
infusion pumps and dialysis

Beckman-Coulter
www.beckman.com
clinical laboratory equipment

Chattanooga
www.chattgroup.com
physical therapy equipment

Datascope
www.datascope.com
patient monitoring

Dräger Medical
www.nad.com
anesthesia and ventilators

Fresenius Medical Care North America
www.fmcna.com
dialysis equipment and dialysis centers

GE Healthcare
www.gehealthcare.com
imaging, patient monitoring, cardiology and
infant care

Getinge USA
www.getinge.com
sterilizers

Hologic
www.hologic.com
mammography and other imaging equipment
focused on women's health

Intuitive Surgical
www.intuitivesurgical.com
robotic surgery

Medison USA
www.medisonusa.com
diagnostic ultrasound equipment

Nihon Kohden
www.nihonkohden.com
patient monitoring

Philips Medical Systems
www.medical.philips.com
imaging, patient monitoring, defibrillation and ECG

Physio-Control
www.physio-control.com
defibrillation

Puritan Bennett
www.puritanbennett.com
ventilators

Siemens Medical
www.medical.siemens.com
imaging, patient monitoring, ventilation and
anesthesia

Spacelabs
www.spacelabs.com
patient monitoring

Toshiba
www.toshiba.com/tams
imaging

Valleylab
www.valleylab.com
electrosurgery

Biomedical Test Equipment Manufacturers & Distributors

BC Group
www.onestopbiomedshop.com

Clinical Dynamics
www.clinicaldynamics.com

Dale Technology
www.daletech.com

Fluke Biomedical
www.flukebiomedical.com

Netech
www.gonetech.com

Pronk Technologies
www.pronktech.com

Rigel Medical
www.rigelmedical.com

Medical Equipment Service Industry Recruiters

Adel-Lawrence Associates
www.adel-lawrence.com

Dick Berg and Associates
www.dickberg.com

Emcon CMA
www.emcon298.com

Stephens International
www.bmets-usa.com

BMET Associations

International Associations

Institute of Biomedical Engineering Technology
http://ibet.asttbc.org/

Clinical Engineering Association of South Africa
http://www.ceasa-national.org.za/

Medical Devices in Scotland
http://www.mdis.org/

Mexican Society of Biomedical Engineering
http://www.somib.org.mx/

National Associations

American College of Clinical Engineering
www.accenet.org

American Society for Healthcare Engineering
www.ashe.org

Association for the Advancement of Medical
Instrumentation (AAMI)
www.aami.org

Healthcare Information and Management Systems
Society
www.himss.org

Medical Equipment and Technology Association
www.mymeta.org

Radiological Society of North America
www.rsna.org

Regional Associations

Biomedical Associations of Wisconsin
www.baw.org

Baltimore Medical Engineers and Technicians Society
www.bmets.org

Biomedical Equipment Society of Texoma, Texas
www.bestbmet.com

California Medical Instrumentation Society
www.cmia.org

Clinical Engineering Association of Illinois
http://www.ceaiweb.org/

Colorado Association of Biomedical Equipment
Technicians
www.cabmet.org

East Tennessee Biomedical Association
http://welcome.to/etba

Florida Biomedical Society
http://www.florida-biomed-society.org/

Georgia Biomedical Instrumentation Society
http://gbisonline.org/

Heartland Biomedical Association
http://hba1.netfirms.com/

Indiana Biomedical Society
http://www.indianabiomedical.com/

Middle Tennessee Biomedical Association
http://www.geocities.com/midtenbiomed/index.html

National Capital Healthcare Engineering Society
http://www.nches.org/

New England Society of Clinical Engineering
http://www.nesce.org/

North Carolina Biomedical Association
http://www.ncbiomedassoc.com/

North Central Biomedical Association
http://www.ncbiomed.org/

North Texas Biomedical Association
http://www.ntba.org

Northern New England Society of Biomedical
Technology
http://www.mv.com/ipusers/nnesbt/NNESBT/Home_
Pagex.html

Ohio Clinical Engineering Association
http://www.ohiocea.org/

Oklahoma Association of Healthcare Engineers
http://www.okahe.org/

Orange County BMET Society
www.ocbmet.com

Philadelphia Area Medical Instrumentation
Association
http://www.pamia.org

SouthEast Texas Clinical Engineering Society
www.setces.org

Virginia Biomedical Association
http://vabiomed.org/index.htm

Washington State Biomedical Association
http://www.bmet.org/

BMET Industry Publications

24 x 7
www.24x7mag.com

Advanced Imaging Magazine
www.advancedimagingpro.com

Biomedical Instrumentation and Technology
(for AAMI members)
www.aami.org

Diagnostic Imaging
www.diagnosticimaging.com

Fierce HealthIT
www.fiercehealthit.com

Health Imaging and IT
www.healthimaging.com

Healthcare IT News
www.healthcareitnews.com

Medical Equipment Dealer
www.mdpublishing

Medical Imaging
www.medicalimagingmag.com

Network World
www.networkworld.com

RFID Journal
www.rfidjournal.com

RT for Decision Makers
www.rtmagazine.com

Additional Suggested Resources

www.auntminnie.com
radiology and imaging news

biomedlinks.com
links to other sites

bmetsonline.org
biomed listserv and other resources

cancerweb.ncl.ac.uk/omd
online medical dictionary

www.clubpacs.com
information on PACS

www.cs.amedd.army.mil/bmet/
DoD biomedical technician training school

www.d-m.com/network.htm
short network tutorial

www.ditecnet.com
medical imaging service training

www.dotmed.com
medical equipment sales, services and news Website

www.ebme.co.uk
European site with BMET-related articles

www.ecri.org
Emergency Care Research Institute, a non-profit
health services research agency

www.fda.gov/cdrh/medicaldevicesafety/
FDA medical device safety

www.innerbody.com/htm/body.html
human anatomy online

www.internationalaid.org
worldwide supplier of medical equipment aid and
training to developing countries

www.jointcommission.org
The Joint Commission (formerly JCAHO)

www.lantronix.com/learning/net-tutor-etntba.html
network tutorials

www.learnthat.com/certification/category-39
free tutorials for A+ and Network+ certifications

www.medhunters.com
jobs and interesting healthcare articles

www.medisend.org
international biomedical equipment technician
training provider

neuro-www.mgh.Harvard.edu/hospitalweb.shtml
U.S. and global hospitals and other Website links

www.or-live.com
live and on-demand Webcasts

www.orbis.org
ORBIS DC-10 "Flying Eye Hospital"

www.otechimg.com
PACS Training

www.quintcareers.com/resume_tutorial
resume tutorial

www.rsti-training.com
medical imaging service training

www.sprawls.org
Sprawls Educational Foundation, has excellent
imaging tutorials

www.williamson-labs.com
variety of tutorials

INDEX

A

Association for the
Advancement of Medical
  Instrumentation (AAMI), 56,
  58, 96
associations. See trade
associations

B

biomedical equipment
technicians (BMETs)
  career paths, 10-12
  certification, 48-55
  computerization of
    equipment, 21, 26-28
  degree programs, 39-45
  education, 37-45
  employers, 17-22
  employment outlook, 4,6
  history of field, 2
  job duties, 13-15
  job titles, 11-12
  necessary skill sets, 23-34
  number of technicians in
    U.S., 3
  overview, 1-3
  salary range and benefits,
    7-9
  why a rewarding field, 3
  work schedules, 15-16
biomedical test equipment
  manufacturers &
    distributors, 95
BMET. See biomedical
equipment technicians

C

Caldwell Community College
(Hudson, NC)
  course outline, 84-85
  two-year degree program,
    84-85
career paths, 10-12
  ISOs, 11, 19, 91-92
  specialization, 10-12
CBET certification, 51-53
  eligibility requirements, 51
  requirements to take exam,
    52
certification, 48-55. See also
education
  benefits of, 48
  BMET certification, 48
  CBET certification, 51-53
  CLES certification, 51, 52
  CompTIA, 54
  computer certifications, 54-
    55
  CRES certification, 51, 52
  dialysis certification, 53
  MSCE (Microsoft), 55
  organizations, 48
computers and computer
networking
  computer certifications, 54-
    55
  necessary skillset, 26-28, 37
customer service skills, 13,
  15, 31-32

D

degree programs. See also education
  accreditation associations, 42-43
  Caldwell Community College (NC), 84-85
  four-year bachelor's degree, 39, 42-43
  Indiana University Purdue University (IN), 85-90
  inverted degrees, 41, 45
  list of degree programs by state, 61-78
  Texas State Technical College (TX), 55-56, 79-83
  two-year associate degree, 39, 41
dialysis certification, 53
DICOM, 31

E-F

education. See also certification; degree programs
  continuing education, 6, 57-59
  development of, 37
  educational requirements, 39
  four-year bachelor's degree, 39, 42-43
  list of degree programs in the U.S., 61-78
  tuition and fees, 44-45
  two-year associate degree, 39, 41

employers, 17-22
  in-house, 18-19
  ISOs (independent service organizations), 19
  OEMs (original equipment manufacturers), 19-20
  profile of, 20-22
  what they are looking for, 17-18
employment outlook, 4, 6
  why a growing field, 4
field service representatives, 16

I

in-house biomedical/ engineering departments, 92
Indiana University Purdue University (IN), 85-90
  Biomedical Engineering Technology, 86
  course outline, 86-89
  distance learning, 85-86, 90
ISOs (independent service organizations), 11, 19
  examples of large, 19
  list of, 91-92

J

job duties, 13-15
  customer service, 13, 15
  other duties, 14
  preventative maintenance and repair, 13-15
  train staff, 13
job titles, 11-12
  modalities, 11-12

specialization, 11-12

M

manufacturers of medical equipment
industry recruiters, 95
list of, 92-94
training on equipment, 58-59
medical equipment, 29-31
C arm, 46
CT scanner, 22
defibrillator, 50, 57
electrical safety analyzer, 24
history of, 1-2
infusion pump, 10, 60
MRI, 35
patient monitor, 16, 59
safety, 29-30
ventilator, 6, 36
X-ray machine, 32, 48
Medical Equipment and Technology Association, 58, 96
medical equipment service industry recruiters, 95
medical imaging specialists, 17
necessary skillset, 30-31
salary expectations, 7

O-P
OEMs (original equipment manufacturers), 19-20
examples of, 20
people skills, 15, 31-32, 43
Picture Archiving and Communication Systems (PACS), 11
professionalism, 32, 34, 37, 47
profiles of biomedical technicians
Andrews, Billy, 12-13
Bowles, Roger (author), 55-56, 107
Brinkley, Eric, 53-54
Christe, Barbara, 41-42
Davis, Robert, 4-6
Dutton, Thomas, 39-40
Fleming, Heather, 9-10
Hargraves, Letha, 43
Noblitt, John, 37, 46-47
Rushing, Bradley, 38-39
Swartz, Ken, 30-31
Sovocool, Scott, 20-22
Stiles, Andrew, 25-26
Tow, Kenneth, 49

R
resources, 91-102
in-house biomedical departments, 92
independent service organizations (ISOs), 91-92
medical equipment manufacturers, 92-94
medical equipment service industry recruiters, 95
misc., 100-102
trade associations, 96-99
trade journals, 56, 57, 58, 99-100

S

safety
  electro-medical equipment,
  2-3
  understanding of, 29-30
salary range, 7-10
  benefits, 8-9
  entry-level technicians, 7
  experienced, 7
  on-call pay, 8
skillset and knowledge
(necessary)
  anatomy & physiology, 24-
  25
  communication skills, 17,
  18, 31, 33
  computers & computer
  networking, 26-28, 37
  customer service, 13, 15,
  31-32
  critical thinking, 49
  electronics, 23
  good "shop skills," 33-34
  medical equipment, 29
  medical terminology, 24-25
  people skills, 15, 31-32, 43
  professionalism, 32, 34, 37,
  47
  safety, 29-30
  self-starter, 18
  teamwork, 18, 47
  time management, 34
  troubleshooting, 27, 28
stress on the job, 9, 31-32, 47

T
telemetry, 40

Texas State Technical College
(Waco,TX), 55-56
  course outline, 80-83
  degree programs (two and
  four year), 79-83
  overview of, 79-80
trade associations, 56, 58
  international, 96
  national, 96
  regional, 97-99
trade journals, 56, 57, 58, 99-
100
troubleshooting equipment,
27, 28

W-X-Y-Z

Notes

Notes

Notes

Notes

About the Author

Roger Bowles

Dr. Bowles began at Texas State Technical College Waco as a student in the Biomedical Equipment Technology until 1991. He went to work at Methodist Hospitals of Dallas after graduation. In 1995, he moved to Pennsylvania and worked for the Reading Hospital and Medical Center in Reading, PA, until 1997. Bowles accepted the position of instructor at TSTC Waco in June of 1997. By that time, he was ready for warmer weather.

Dr. Bowles says that "Critical Careers", published in 2001, was sorely in need of updating and is no longer in print. Instructors needed a book that could be used in the Intro to Biomedical Equipment Technology course as an overview of the field. This book serves as that purpose and also explains, the working conditions, the different career paths available and provides some insight into the daily life of a biomedical equipment technician. Dr. Bowles hopes this book will serve as a source of information to attract people to the field.

TSTC Publishing

Established in 2004, TSTC Publishing is a provider of high-end technical instructional materials and related information to institutions of higher education and private industry. "High end" refers simultaneously to the information delivered, the various delivery formats of that information, and the marketing of materials produced. More information about the products and services offered by TSTC Publishing may be found at its Web site: http://publishing.tstc. edu/.